CONDITIONS OF LIBERTY

CONDITIONS OF LIBERTY

CIVIL SOCIETY AND ITS RIVALS

Ernest Gellner

ALLEN LANE
THE PENGUIN PRESS

ALLEN LANE
THE PENGUIN PRESS

Published by the Penguin Group
Penguin Books USA Inc., 375 Hudson Street, New York, New York 10014, USA
Penguin Books Ltd, 27 Wrights Lane, London w8 5tz, England
Penguin Books Australia Ltd, Ringwood, Victoria, Australia
Penguin Books Canada Ltd, 10 Alcorn Avenue, Toronto, Ontario, Canada m4v 3b2
Penguin Books (NZ) Ltd, 182–190 Wairau Road, Auckland 10, New Zealand

Penguin Books Ltd, Registered Offices: Harmondsworth, Middlesex, England

First American edition
Published in 1994 by Viking Penguin,
a division of Penguin Books USA Inc.

3 5 7 9 10 8 6 4 2

Copyright © Ernest Gellner, 1994
All rights reserved.

ISBN 0–7139–9114–3

CIP data available

Printed in England by Clays Ltd, St Ives plc
Set in 11.5/14 pt Monophoto Bembo

To Lena and Yura Senokosov

CONTENTS

ACKNOWLEDGEMENTS

During the period of work on this book, I received financial support from the Economic and Social Research Council and from the Nuffield Foundation, and I wish to express my gratitude to Sir Douglas Hague (erstwhile Chairman of the ESRC) and to Miss Patricia Thomas, Assistant Director of the Foundation, for their confidence. It made a great difference.

The work on this book was begun while I was still a member of the Social Anthropology Department at the University of Cambridge. Very many of its members helped me in diverse ways, but very special gratitude is due to Mary McGinley, Margaret Story and Humphrey Hinton.

The book was completed while I was working at the Central European University, Prague, and its Centre for the Study of Nationalism. There, too, very many people helped me during the period of completion of the book, but I ought to mention quite particularly Robin Cassling, Vlasta Hirtová and Monica Pospíšilová. Gaye Woolven was an admirable editor and she was greatly helped by Bela Cunha and Keith Taylor. Wendy Fitzpatrick assisted with the page proofs. Among the office holders of the CEU to whom I am particularly indebted for providing a framework in which it was possible to work, I should mention Jiří Musil, Anne Lonsdale, George Soros, Alf Stepan and Claire Wallace. In the wider world, my debts to John Hall and Ian Jarvie are especially great. The defects of the book are my own.

Ernest Gellner
Centre for the Study of Nationalism
Central European University
Prague
June 1994

A SLOGAN IS BORN

A new ideal was born, or reborn, in recent decades: Civil Society. Previously, a person interested in the notion of Civil Society could be assumed to be a historian of ideas, concerned perhaps with Locke or Hegel. But the phrase itself had no living resonance or evocativeness. Rather, it seemed distinctly covered with dust. And now, all of a sudden, it has been taken out and thoroughly dusted, and has become a shining emblem.

There is relatively little mystery concerning why this should have happened. The condition defined by this term had become highly valued and loaded with political appeal. In extensive parts of the world, what it denoted was absent. This lack came in due course to be strongly felt and bitterly resented: eventually it turned into an aching void. The absence was felt acutely in societies which had strongly centralized all aspects of life, and where a single political-economic-ideological hierarchy tolerated no rivals and one single vision defined not only truth but also personal rectitude. This caused the rest of society to approximate an atomized condition, and dissent then became a mark of heresy or, in the terminology of modern ideocracy, it defined an 'enemy of the people'.

Societies of this kind had emerged through the influence and the implementation of Marxism, and one way of summarizing the central intuition of Marxism is to say: Civil Society is a fraud. The idea of a plurality of institutions – both opposing and balancing the state, and in turn controlled and protected by the state – is, in the Marxist view, merely the provision of a façade for a hidden and maleficent domination. It helps to reinforce such a domination by coercive institutions masquerading as benign, neutral or divinely ordained. Marxism claims to unmask both partners in this deception – the state which protects Civil Society, and Civil Society which provides a counterweight to the state. Both are damned as redundant and fraudulent.

So, it was claimed, there is no need for such a formula: once exploitation comes to an end, a social order will emerge which will have no need of coercive reinforcement. Only a pathological internal division of society created the need for a state; the overcoming of that condition automatically renders the state redundant. There will be no need for a state, and so naturally there will also be no need for additional institutions to counterbalance that central agency of order.

On this view the whole cluster of ideas associated with the phrase Civil Society stands for something which is both spurious and unnecessary. A harmonious social order, free of both exploitation and oppression, is possible after all. The formula for its construction is available. Its realization is on the agenda of history, and its coming will be ensured both by the inner logic of events and by the iron will of the quasi-religious order devoted to its implementation.

The actual experience of societies endeavouring to implement this vision in the end also conclusively undermined it. The first attempt at liberalizing Communist societies after the death of Stalin and in the course of the Khrushchevian thaw was, indeed, still marked by a retention of the original faith, and a desire to free it from its alleged 'deformations'. The central idea remained valid, it was felt, and only its implementation had gone astray. If there was a dominant slogan accompanying the reforms of that period within Marxist societies, it was 'alienation'. The same term also provided a focus for the intellectual activity of those in the West eager to endow Marxism with a new life and a fresh, moralistic image. The works of the young Marx, including parts of which he himself had later come to be ashamed and had never published, were revived with a view to offering a formulation of Marxism which was moralistic rather than scientistic, and which could provide a standard for judging and correcting faulty implementation of Marxism (a danger previously not seriously considered). The moral inspiration and aspiration of Marxism was stressed more than its scientistic pretensions. There was still the belief that, technically, Communism could be and would be effective, and that, morally, if only it was purged of its deformations, it could be admirable.

By the time of the second liberalization under Gorbachev, nothing remained of either of these two illusions. The second liberalization had been provoked and rendered necessary by an indisputable, and no longer disputed, technical failure and inferiority. As for moral superiority, strangely enough the sleazy but at least relatively mild squalor of the Brezhnev years proved far more corrosive for the image of the faith than the total, pervasive, random and massively destructive terror of Stalinism. That terror could at least be seen as the fearful but appropriately dramatic heralding of a totally new social order, the coming of a new man. It was indeed frequently seen in such a light. It was somehow fitting that the coming of a new humanity would be sanctified by so much blood. The squalor, on the other hand, heralded nothing at all except, perhaps, more squalor. It is possible to live with squalor, especially if the regime guilty of it is also relatively tolerant of those who do not actively oppose or threaten the system, but it hardly heralds a new dawn for mankind.

Now a new ideal or counter-vision, or at least a slogan-contrast, was required, and appropriately enough it was found in Civil Society, in the idea of institutional and ideological pluralism, which prevents the establishment of monopoly of power and truth, and counterbalances those central institutions which, though necessary, might otherwise acquire such monopoly. The actual practice of Marxism had led, wherever it came to be implemented, to what might be called Caesaro-Papism-Mammonism, to the near-total fusion of the political, ideological and economic hierarchies. The state, the church-party and the economic managers were all parts of one single *nomenklatura*. A single and centralized hierarchy with an unambiguous apex monopolized all important decisions. Autonomy of the formal segments, consultation and electoral decision-taking were all of them pure theatre, and known to be such. This tendency was perhaps specially marked in a society which had in any case been, even prior to the coming of Marxism, strongly Caesaro-Papist. The superimposition of Marxism on Byzantine theology and traditions proved disastrous. Modern administrative and communication technology had made economic centralization both more feasible and more disastrous than it had been in the days when Russian villages were isolated by impassable mud in spring and autumn, and when nature herself, if not human will, had circumscribed autocracy. Modern technology at the service of Caesaro-Papism did not shine in economic performance, but it endowed authoritarianism with an altogether new, totalitarian quality.

By the 1980s if not before, the consequences of such a system had become plain for all to see. Economically it was disastrous, and had caused the Soviet Union to be beaten simultaneously in the consumerist and in the arms race. It was bad enough for a country to have a Chayanovite peasantry and working class – one preferring security to increased output, as the Russian economist Chayanov had shown – but the unification of all hierarchies also led to a Chayanovite bureaucracy, one playing politics and playing safe, rather than committed to effectiveness. Its members were inevitably far more concerned with their position

4

inside the networks than they were with technical efficiency, which would earn them no good marks and was indeed liable to earn them black ones. They learnt how to cheat the plan rather than how to increase output. Excessive zeal for production would cause friction, and might well earn a person guilty of it the label of saboteur.

At the same time, the system led to an atomized, individualized society, where it was barely possible – or literally not possible at all – to found a philatelic club without political supervision. Far from creating a new social man, one freed from egotistic greed, commodity fetishism and competitiveness, which had been the Marxist hope, the system created isolated, amoral, cynical individualists-without-opportunity, skilled at double-talk and trimming within the system, but incapable of effective enterprise. In these circumstances, the very thing which Marxism had proclaimed to be a fraud was suddenly seen to be something that was to be most ardently desired. The dusty term, drawn from antiquated political theory, belonging to long, obscure and justly forgotten debates, re-emerged, suddenly endowed with a new and powerful capacity to stir enthusiasm and inspire action.

What is it?

The simplest, immediate and intuitively obvious definition, which also has a good deal of merit, is that Civil Society is that set of diverse non-governmental institutions which is strong enough to counterbalance the state and, while not preventing the state from fulfilling its role of keeper of the peace and arbitrator between major interests, can nevertheless prevent it from dominating and atomizing the rest of society.

Such a definition conveys the idea contained in the phrase, and also highlights the reason for the newly emerged attractiveness of the slogan. None the less, this definition has a grave deficiency. It is good as far as it goes, but it does not go far enough. The problem is simple: such a definition would include under the notion of 'Civil Society' many forms of social order which would not satisfy *us*.

The point is this: historically, mankind has not always suffered under centralized despotism. It has suffered from it frequently, more often than not perhaps, but not everywhere and at all times; quite frequently it was free from such oppression.

The imposition of a despotism is not always an easy matter. Pre-modern polities quite often lack the equipment for pulverizing and then dominating the societies they control. They are interested in extracting as much surplus as possible and ensuring obedience, but frequently the best way of doing this is to allow local communities to administer themselves, and merely oblige them to supply produce – or labour – on pain of punishment. In circumstances favourable to them, such as those conducive to mobile pastoralism or prevailing in difficult mountainous terrain, local communities can even become fully independent and effectively resist demands for taxation or corvée. In most places in the agrarian world, however, power is concentrated in one dominant and, by our standards, oppressive centre.

The logic of successive elimination of rival candidates for power until one only remains, does indeed operate in certain widely prevalent conditions, such as river valleys. In places where the vanquished cannot escape (because they depend for their survival on immobile fields, for instance), but can be deprived of arms, it then leads to a marked concentration of power and to exploitation. But these conditions do not prevail everywhere. What all this means is that in the traditional agrarian world, though its polities are most often monarchical, one nevertheless often finds internally well-organized, self-administering and partly or wholly autonomous sub-communities.

These, however, maintain their cohesion, internal discipline and solidarity with the help of much ritual, employed to underscore and enforce social roles and obligations. The social roles are generally conceived and defined in kin terms, and may indeed frequently be filled in terms of the kin positions of their occupants. So political, economic, ritual and any other kinds of obligations are superimposed on each other in a single idiom. This strengthens all of them: one cannot ignore one's kin of obligation, for instance, without imperilling other relationships. The price of such strengthening is of course that all spheres of life become rigid, and innovation, technical or other, is rendered that much harder. The social visibility and authority of relationships is fortified by a plethora of ritual reminders: as in a military organization, discipline is enforced by a proliferation of minor rules and hence additional possible transgressions, the avoidance of which puts a heavy and constant burden on each individual, and thus keeps him in awe of the social order as a whole. There are so many ways of putting a foot wrong that a man is always at risk and seldom socially innocent. This being so, he needs to maintain a fund of good will among his fellows and his superiors, to compensate for the transgressions which he cannot but commit, and which render him perpetually vulnerable. His role is stable and ritually orchestrated. It is both internalized and externalized: it enters deep into his soul, and a plethora of markers pervades the outward life of the community. It endows him with an identity both secure and inescapable. He knows only too well who he is and what is expected of him: his prospects of redefining his own identity are negligible.

Traditional man can sometimes escape the tyranny of kings, but only at the cost of falling under the tyranny of cousins, and of ritual. The kin-defined, ritually orchestrated, severely demanding and life-pervading systems of the 'ancient city',[1] in Fustel de Coulanges's sense, may indeed succeed at least for a time in avoiding tyrannical centralization, but only at the cost of a most demanding culture, one

7

which modern man would find intolerably stifling. Roughly, the general sociological law of agrarian society states that man must be subject to either kings or cousins, though quite often, of course, he is subject to both. Kings generally dominate societies through the intermediary of local institutions and communities, so that a tyrant at the centre is sustained by local institutions, and vice versa.

Therefore, if we are to define our notion of Civil Society effectively, we must first of all distinguish it from something which may in itself be attractive or repulsive, or perhaps both, but which is radically distinct from it: the segmentary community which avoids central tyranny by firmly turning the individual into an integral part of the social sub-unit. Romantics feel nostalgia for it and modern individualists may loathe it; but what concerns us here is that, whatever our feelings for it may be, it is very, very different from our notion of Civil Society, even though it satisfies that plausible initial definition of it. It may, indeed, be pluralistic and centralization-resistant, but it does not confer on its members the kind of freedom *we* require and expect from Civil Society.

Fustel de Coulanges in his *La Cité Antique* did more than perhaps anyone else to establish this distinction. His aim was to disabuse his fellow French citizens, who had for some time been eager to invoke the alleged liberties of the ancients as precedents for the liberties they were eager to acquire or to fortify in their own society. But this was a total misunderstanding, Fustel claimed:

L'idée que l'on s'est faite de la Grèce et de Rome a souvent troublé nos générations. Pour avoir mal observé les institutions de la cité ancienne, on a imaginé de les faire revivre chez nous. On s'est fait illusion sur la liberté chez les anciens et pour cela seul la liberté chez les modernes a été mise en péril.[2]

Fustel was eager to cure his compatriots of their illusions, and thereby guard against the dangers inherent in them. Fustel was anticipated on this point by Benjamin Constant[3] who, however, only pointed out the absence of individual freedom among the ancients (even when they enjoyed liberty in the sense that their city was free of a tyrant or of foreign domination). He did not see, or at any rate he did not firmly point out, the role of social sub-groups and of ritual in the subjugation of the individual. So he cannot altogether be claimed as an ancestor of the Durkheimian sociological and anthropological tradition, and hence of the understanding of a kind of society which, though plural, does not resemble our Civil Society.

Segmentary communities constitute an important social form, but it is one which differs significantly both from centralized tyrannies and from our Civil Society. Nor can Constant really be hailed as the anticipator of the distinction between 'positive' and 'negative' liberty. The objection to the ancient city is not so much that it prefers positive liberty (fulfilment) to negative liberty (absence of external constraints), but that its crucial defects preclude the possibility of formulating this contrast. It thrusts on to the individual an ascribed identity, which then may or may not be fulfilled, whereas a modern conception of freedom includes the requirement that identities be chosen rather than ascribed.

This particular danger of confusing modern and ancient liberty may not be serious in our time: the rhetoric of the recent converts to the idea of Civil Society does not contain much, if indeed it contains any, invocation of the ancient liberties of the Greeks and Romans. Pericles was not invoked, nor Plutarch quoted, by striking dockyard workers or miners in Gdansk or Donetz. Nevertheless, a proper understanding of what the ideal of Civil Society really means *now* must distinguish it from an implicit identification with any and every plural society, within which well-established institutions counterbalance the state. That is simply too broad. The danger of such a mistake is present in current discourse if it adopts the intuitively plausible definition of Civil Society which already takes for granted a modern context and, so, tacitly excludes ancient pluralism. But, unless 'segmentary' societies are clearly excluded, the definition of Civil Society invoked at the start includes them, and mistakenly identifies them with what we want now. But such an equation is not merely in error theoretically, it also has practical consequences. These, even if they are not the same as those of the French contemporaries and predecessors of Fustel, are important.

Fustel is exceedingly eloquent on the matter of how much real individual liberty in the modern sense there was in the ancient city:

> La cité avait été fondée sur une religion et constituée comme une Eglise. De là sa force; de là aussi son omnipotence et l'empire absolu qu'elle exerçait sur ses membres. Dans une société établie sur de tels principes, la liberté individuelle ne pouvait pas exister. Le citoyen était soumis en toutes choses et sans aucune reserve à la cité . . . La vie privée n'échappait pas à cette omnipotence de l'Etat . . . Il exerçait sa tyrannie jusque dans les plus petites choses . . .[4]

Fustel was concerned to show how this kind of plural, non-centralized, but socially oppressive society, despite its political pluralism could never satisfy a modern craving for Civil Society. It was eventually replaced by a new order, one in which the Christian separation of religion and polity made individual liberty thinkable. In this way, Fustel was not merely the ancestor of those who, like L. Dumont,[5] try to locate the religious origins of Western individualism, but also of those who seek to understand the kind of society based on the principles he had laid bare, and which in due course was to be called 'segmentary'. Fustel's story recorded the disappearance and replacement of one set of such societies, those of classical antiquity. In fact they had not disappeared from the earth, or even from the Mediterranean. They are a hardy plant, which is part of the reason why they merit attention.

Fustel and his ideas have thus also become the inspiration of those many investigators, who have since come to be called social anthropologists, who are eager to understand societies which long continued to function in the manner which Fustel credited primarily to Mediterranean antiquity. In his own time, Emile Masqueray rediscovered the ancient city, under Muslim camouflage, in the Berber hills of Algeria.[6] For some reason which might repay investigation, the great Parisian star Fustel and the provincial nobody Masqueray coldly and almost completely ignored each other, though they must have known each other and their paths had crossed: Masqueray's scheme of evolution of Berber communities in Algeria mirrored Fustel's triadic succession in the ancient Mediterranean. Was it general or academic politics which explains this mutual avoidance by the two men? More recently, an American scholar has used Fustel, directly rather than mediated by Durkheim as is more common, in studying a long-urbanized and unusual Asian population, the Nepalese Newars. After summarizing Fustel's segmentary account of society and the way in which each level of segments was sustained by its deities and rites, Robert Levy goes on to comment:

> Fustel's portrait contained a deeply felt myth, that of an earthly paradise of orderly, family-based unities prior to a transformation into a larger, impersonal and conflict-ridden state organisation.[7]

Perhaps Fustel's materials were indeed used to help foster such a myth, though Fustel himself was rather concerned, as we have seen, to counter an earlier myth, that of the ancient city as a precursor or model of the French Revolution and its ideals.

But the real situation is at the very least triangular (later we may need to add further options): there are the segmentary communities, cousin-ridden and ritual-ridden, free perhaps of central tyranny, but not really free in a sense that would satisfy us; there is centralization which grinds into the dust all subsidiary social institutions or sub-communities, whether ritually stifling or not; and finally, there is the third alternative we seek to define and attain. It excludes both stifling communalism and centralized authoritarianism. It is *this* kind of Civil Society which concerns us.

A proper definition of it must take all this into account: Civil Society has at the very least two contrasts, and so its essence cannot be seized with the help of a merely bi-polar opposition between pluralism and monocentrism. We must try to understand that which we have suddenly discovered we possess and value. Many of us in the West took it for granted (some still do), as a kind of normal human condition, while those in the East learnt to love it more ardently by being so thoroughly deprived of it, and by seeing the utter falsity of the faith which declared it to be redundant and fraudulent. But we need to know just what it is we love. We can only identify it through characterizing the full variety of its historic contrasts.[8]

THE TWO NEIGHBOURS

Atlantic society is endowed with Civil Society, and on the whole, at any rate since 1945, it has enjoyed it without giving it much or any thought. Much contemporary social theory takes it for granted in an almost comical manner: it simply starts out with the assumption of an unconstrained and secular individual, unhampered by social or theological bonds, freely choosing his aims, and reaching some agreement concerning social order with his fellows. In this manner, Civil Society is simply presupposed as some kind of inherent attribute of the human condition! It is the corollary of a certain vision of man. It is a naïve universalization of one rather fortunate kind of man – the inhabitant of Civil Society. In reality, he is radically distinct from members of other kinds of society. He is not *man-as-such*.

It is only the rediscovery of this ideal in Eastern Europe in the course of the last two decades that has reminded the inhabitants of the liberal states on either shore of the northern Atlantic of just what it is that they possess and ought to hold dear. We are reminded of it above all by East Europeans who have found a name for what they in turn sorely miss. But having become aware of it, we should also notice that this liberal civilization possessed on its eastern and south-eastern borders two rather different kinds of neighbour.

Each of these neighbours has at times been a source of grave problems, sometimes simultaneously. In 1956, the West allowed its preoccupation with the real or imagined danger of Nasser to give second place to the issue of the repression of Magyar liberty (though admittedly, it is less than clear just what the West could possibly have done at that time, had its priorities been different). By contrast, in

1990, it was precisely the marked improvement of relations with the north-eastern neighbours which enabled the West to be so incomparably more effective in the Middle East than it had been in 1956. Saddam, unlike Nasser, was not able to profit from a European confrontation synchronized with his own aggression.

As became manifest in the course of the late 1980s, leading up to its subsequent disintegration, the Marxist world was marked by an almost total loss of faith in its own erstwhile central doctrine, and also by a strong and pervasive yearning for Civil Society. It is in this region after all that the slogan and the ideal were reborn and endowed with a new and vibrant meaning. The Muslim world, by contrast, is marked by the astonishing resilience of its formal faith, and a merely weak, at best, striving for Civil Society. Its absence is not widely felt to be scandalous, and stirs up relatively little local interest. On the contrary, ruthlessly clientelist, winner-takes-all polities are largely taken for granted and accepted as inherent in the nature of things.

In each case, Civil Society is or was conspicuous by its absence. But in one case, there is a strong craving for it, thwarted only or primarily by the inability of the society, at any rate so far, to create the appropriate economic preconditions, whereas in the other case the desire itself is largely, though not wholly, lacking.

A thing is perhaps best understood through its contrasts: and here we have at least two contrasts, quite distinct from each other, of the entity which concerns us. Perhaps it should be approached through looking at each of these oppositions in succession, and combining what we can learn from each.

3

ISLAM

Islam is unique among the major world civilizations or religions. Some four centuries ago at the end of the Middle Ages, the Old World contained four literate higher civilizations, each with its own religion or cluster of religions. As a result of the dramatic history of the subsequent period, three of these are unmistakably, though not uniformly or completely, secularized. The widely held sociological thesis affirming that in industrial or industrializing societies religion loses much of its erstwhile hold over men and society is, by and large, correct. Both the extent and the nature of secularization vary a good deal, and it is certainly less than complete – and there are occasional marked counter-currents. For all that, it would be difficult to deny the overall trend towards secularization.

But there is one marked exception: the world of Islam. The hold of Islam over the populations of the lands in which it is the main religion has in no way diminished in the course of the last hundred years. In some ways it has been markedly strengthened. Moreover, the hold is not restricted to certain layers of society; one cannot say that it is only among the lower classes, the rustics or the women that the faith has retained its vigour. Its hold is as strong among ruling and urban classes and cultural élites as it is among less favoured segments of the population. It is as marked among traditionalist regimes as it is among those committed to social radicalism.

In the main, the West has only noticed the phenomenon since the Iranian revolution, which was indeed its most dramatic though perhaps not its most typical manifestation. There is now a tendency to refer to this phenomenon as 'fundamentalism', but the term is liable to be somewhat misleading. In the West, 'fundamentalists' are those who protect an old and above all literal interpretation of the doctrine of their faith against attempts to reinterpret it as metaphorical, symbolic, social, functional or whatever. These reinterpretations aim to make religion more palatable and digestible to the modern spirit. The fundamentalism which is so pervasive in the Muslim world would no doubt also condemn such watering-down bowdlerizations, but this is not the frontier on which it is most active. The area of dispute in which it does make itself most felt is an old internal division within Islam, long present though not always formally recognized, between what one might call the High and the Low Cultures of Islam. Fundamentalism is indeed opposed to alien un-belief, or to bowdlerizing reinterpretation, but it is also deeply concerned with countering folk distortions of Islam, illegitimate superstitions and ritual accretions.

It is in terms of this old polarity between High and Folk Islam that the persisting vigour is not merely best described, but also best explained. One must begin with the roles of High and Low Islam in traditional Muslim society, i.e. the Muslim world as it was prior to the brutal impact of the West, which made itself felt at different times in different regions between the eighteenth and the twentieth centuries.

Formally, Islam has no clergy. It does not officially separate church from society, any more than it formally separates church from state. It does not possess, as some other civilizations have been said to possess, an exemplary centre holding up the Ideal to man, whether in a political or a religious court. If anyone in practice possesses such a role within Islam, it is the scholars, the theologians–jurists, the *ulama*. But they do not constitute a sacramentally segregated caste or stratum: they can only claim scholarship, familiarity with the scripturally recorded social/legal ideal, and hence the ability and will to practise and implement it, and no more. As for political authority, it is charged with enforcing divine law, rather than specifically or paradigmatically exemplifying it, let alone creating it. It must *observe* it, as must others, but it does not inherently constitute either its source or its norm.

This, of course, is of great importance in a scripturalist religion, a faith which holds that the divine message, literally, is available to mankind in writing. It is also important in a religion which holds that the divine truth is not only a matter of doctrine about the nature of the world, but also, and perhaps primarily, a matter of quite detailed law concerning the conduct of life and society. As the Orientalist Michael Cook pointed out, Islam combines the theocentrism of Christianity with the legalism of Judaism. The result is a legal blueprint of social order, which stands above mere power and political authority. This transcendent Law, when not actually found in the original and severely finite and circumscribed Message, is to be found in its written elaborations by competent scholars, plus Traditions putatively originating in the Messenger and the precepts and example left by Him and his Companions. They, in principle, constitute the normative Model. It is linked to a recorded message and to inferences from it, and not to political authority as such. The availability of all this important, indeed crucial, information-in-writing inevitably enhances the social importance of the men who can read, scholars, men of learning. Long before the formulation of the modern ideals of the Separation of Powers and an entrenched Constitution, Islam in effect possessed a religious version of both: legislation was distinct from the executive because it had been pre-empted by the deity, and religion itself was above all the Constitutional Law of society.

Scholars, often of urban background and rooted in the trading bourgeoisie of the towns, project a corresponding vision of the faith – scripturalist, rule-oriented, puritanical, literal, sober, egalitarian, anti-ecstatic. Perhaps such a religious style comes naturally to men of scholarly temperament, and perhaps it also corresponds to the values and life-style of the commercial urban class from which they sprang.

Be that as it may, such a religious style does *not* correspond very much, or at all, to the natural inclinations or needs of quite extensive other segments of the population. For instance, it does not correspond to the tastes and needs of the rural population, much of which was until recently self-administering through its own local kin or tribal units. Such rural populations are generally illiterate and have little inclination or ability impelling them to devote their spare time to theological or jurisprudential learning. On the other hand, however, they do need ritual specialists to maintain and service periodic rituals, which fortify and define those local groups, which constitute the social framework, and maintain stability and security. In brief, they need a Durkheimian religion, which supplies the social punctuation of time and space. If priests managing this punctuation do not exist, then they must be invented. And so they are.

The most characteristic institution of rural Islam was the saint cult, differing however from the saint cults of, say, the Catholic shore of the Mediterranean, in that the saints were generally *living* personages, performing services here and now, in person, rather than being revered for past sanctity and used for mediation in another world. In Catholicism, dead saints are approachable through living priests. In Folk Islam, saints are (or were) alive and well. Saints were priests. Dead saints could be approached through living saints, in one great partnership of the living, the dead and the yet unborn. They mediated in this world. The network of saints linked past and present, this world and the other, kinship and faith.

Rustic tribal or semi-tribal populations were not the only

ones given to the worship of living saints, saintly lineages and saintly associations (normally appearing in the literature as religious Orders or Fraternities or Brotherhoods). The lower classes of the towns were also liable to look to religion and its practices as an escape from their miserable condition, as a temporary evasion by means of ecstasy induced by mystical technique, drugs, dancing, music, snake-charming, reverence for charismatic personalities, and other stimulants, and conducted under saintly guidance. If the prosperous bourgeoisie looked to scripturalism for a *confirmation* of its comfortable life-style, the lower orders looked to more ecstatic religion for an *escape* from their own miserable condition. The two most popular theories of religion would present it as *opium* or as a *charter*: the two aspects are not fully compatible. The well-heeled favour a charter, and the miserable need a drug. The audio-visual aids of faith were essential for psychic consolation as well as for externalizing the social order.

Scholarship and sober piety may help confirm the more affluent bourgeoisie in its enjoyment of its own privileged condition, but it will not console the less fortunate, who turn to mediators and bringers of ecstasy who provide a more tangible consolation and exciting escape. So the lower-cultural variant of the faith suits not only the rustics, locked in their kin units and requiring that these units be serviced and ritually externalized, but also the more miserable members of the urban population, requiring ritual and excitement as a personal solace rather than as a social lubricant.

One should not give the impression that the two variants of the faith were always clearly and overtly defined, sharply separated, and that they confronted each other in stark opposition. This would be a gross misrepresentation of the situation. Everything was continuous, the transitions were gradual, the boundaries ambiguous and shadowy. This obfuscation of contrasts was itself very useful. The rustics recognized the authority of the High ideal, even if they neither could nor desired to practise it. They often attributed great feats of scholarship to the Founding Saint of their local saintly lineage, even if its current representative had lost all pretensions to any such erudition. Thus they recognized the authority of an ideal which they did not normally even try to implement. Likewise, at the centre, the urban scholar would also generally be a member of a saint cult. This was the concession of the purer ideal to the pervasive weakness of the social will.

The two systems interpenetrated each other in what was for much of the time perfectly amiable symbiosis. But not always. There remained a latent tension which would come to the surface from time to time in the form of a puritan revivalist movement, aiming at transforming the Lower in the image of the Higher, at implementing seriously an ideal which had never been renounced, yet was not properly practised either. These movements triumphed from time to time, though they never succeeded permanently, prior to modern times: the religious will may be strong, but the social flesh is weak. The exigencies of rural life and the psychic needs of urban poverty would in due course lead to the revival of the old practices, the persistent use of magic, ritual and personal mediation. In the traditional order, Islam may be described as a Permanent or Recurrent but ever-reversed Reformation: in each cycle, the Revivalist puritan impulse would in the end yield to the contrary social requirements.

So, in the past, reform was ever cyclical. Social reform using a religious idiom only succeeded, as Friedrich Engels echoing Ibn Khaldun noted, in turning the wheel round full circle, back to its social starting point. Reaffirming the pervasive Eurocentrism of the founding fathers of Marxism, Engels noted that, whereas with the Europeans the religious camouflage of social conflict in the end leads to genuine change, with the Orientals, especially Arabs, it leads to only cyclical mutations which leave the structure intact.[1]

But under modern conditions the rules of the game have changed. The colonial and post-colonial state was in possession of military, communication and transport technology, which at long last undermined and destroyed the autonomy of those rural self-administering units which had previously, throughout the arid zone, successfully defied the central state. The society was now politically centralized and effectively governed from the centre, thus imposing a unified economic system. There was a general atomization of the society, transformed by population explosion, urbanization and urban domination, and greatly increased mobility.

In these circumstances, the old mediator-saints lost most (though not all) of their previous functions: they were no longer required to mediate between social groups, for the groups themselves had been eroded. They could only retain their therapeutic role, especially given the woeful inadequacy of modern medical services. The urbanized, or at any rate de-tribalized and de-ruralized, population aspired to live up to the urban ideals, eager to ratify its promotion from the status of rustic backwardness and ignorance to urban sophistication and propriety, by practising a rule-observing rather than saint-invoking style of faith. How better to demonstrate its ascension than by disavowing those saintly mediators, who had always in theory been heterodox anyway and who now no longer served any useful purpose? When the gendarmerie prevents the activation of clan loyalty to defend a shared pasture or perpetuate a feud, what need is there for a living saint who would mediate between the clans? The avoidance of mediation had in the past been an obligation too difficult to fulfil: now circumstances had made it easy and attractive, indeed both obligatory and feasible, and so one could rejoice in the new-found orthodoxy. The use of mediators no longer being either effective or permitted, it was convenient to heed the old prohibition of mediation. Temptation gone, observance of the High rules became easy and attractive. Puritanism and fundamentalism became tokens of urban sophistication.

This constitutes the basic mechanism of that massive transfer of loyalty away from saint cults towards a scripturalist, 'fundamentalist' variant of Islam. This is the essence of the cultural history of Islam of the last hundred years. What had once been a minority accomplishment or privilege, a form of the faith practised by a cultural élite, has now come to define the society as a whole.

The essence of nationalism in the West is that a High – literacy-linked – culture becomes the pervasive, membership-defining culture of the total society; the same has happened in Islam, but it expresses itself in fundamentalism rather than nationalism, though the two are sometimes conflated. For the masses, the High form of Islam ratified their move to urban status, it defined them against the foreigner whom they encountered in the colonial conflict – the new colonial nation was often simply the sum total of Muslims in arbitrarily defined territory, which previously knew no collective identity – and it also provided them with a kind of charter, a moral entrenched constitution, against their own newly emerging, morally often suspect, technocratic leadership. This is, of course, a function the faith had long performed in Islam. If the ruled judged their rulers, they did so by applying the religious norms of sacred law, rather than the secular principles of a Civil Society. Severe and fastidious about the implementation of the sacred prescriptions, they are not otherwise over-sensitive about the internal organization of political authority, nor greatly perturbed by its clientelist structure and its unfastidious methods and partiality. Nothing else is expected of politics. Authority is accountable to God for implementation of religious-legal rules, but not to man for the practice of some civil ideal. Only the tribes had practised participatory politics at home, but, if anything, they had given it a bad name by linking it to moral and religious laxity. Their secular custom expresses a general will, but it is morally suspect as a deviation from the divine will.

This collective self-identification in terms of the erstwhile High tradition made possible a remarkable escape from a painful dilemma, which otherwise generally haunts Third World countries. Normally, such societies seek to escape the humiliations of backwardness. The choice they face, given that the weak *ancien régime* and its High culture are discredited, is between either emulating the foreigner ('Westernization'), or idealizing the local folk tradition as the carrier of deep values ('populism'). Muslims are not obliged to do either. They left the idealization of folk culture to foreigners, who romanticized the tribesman in the T.E. Lawrence style. They themselves were able to idealize a local tradition which was indeed genuinely local, but not at all folksy: High Islam may not really be, as its adherents like to think, the perpetuation of the pristine practice of the Prophet and his Companions, but it is something that has genuinely been a prestigious part and parcel of the Muslim civilization for a very long time. It possesses features – scripturalism, puritanism, individualism, rule-orientation, a low loading of magic, an aversion to disorderly folk practices and mystical indulgence – which may have marked elective affinities with the virtues required to surmount the arduousness and strains of the long march to a disciplined, modern, industrial society. It seems almost tailor-made for such a predicament.

If a Muslim society is to reform itself and catch up and acquire international dignity, it seems able to do it in terms of its own old High ideals, rather than in terms of something borrowed from outside or something credited to the pristine folk. Moreover, this puritan, revivalist or fundamentalist

Islam can perform precisely the function which nationalism has performed elsewhere: provide a new self-image for people no longer able to identify with their position in village, lineage, clan or tribe. These groupings no longer operate, and those who leave them are eager to link themselves to a culture which gives them *droit de cité* in a much wider and internally mobile society. The Low Islam of saints confirms a particularistic society; the High Islam of the scholars and rulers defines an anonymous mobile mass society produced by modern conditions. The astonishing Muslim self-reformation of the last hundred years reflects this social change.

It is a paradox that the force of this Muslim current has been noticed by the West mainly as a consequence of the Iranian revolution, given that this revolution is in certain ways rather untypical. In the spectrum represented by Muslim sects (which in some measure cuts across our Low and High Islam distinction), Shi'ism is the variant closest to the cult of personality, as opposed to a religiously more egalitarian cult of the Law. In Shi'ism, the cults of personality and of martyrdom are fused, as they are in Christianity. Shi'ism solved the central problem of religious and political validation – the problem of the regress: who validates the ultimate validation? – by the simple device of postulating absolutely perfect, infallible beings, the sacred Imams, whose existence is co-temporal with the deity itself, and who, in virtue of this status and the inerrancy it entails, can validate the true faith and its correct interpretation. Their perfection guarantees the correctness of interpretation, which consequently does not need to be validated further. In this manner, one escapes the regress of legitimation.

The fact that these ultimate validators are also in hiding, which makes any immediate consultation difficult, both complicates and eases the situation: it is necessary to wait for the Return, and in the meantime make do with makeshift arrangements, which in the past included the acceptance of monarchy, but which now implies what might be called the 'dictatorship of the scholar'. Government is indeed to be carried out not by men but by lawyers. If righteousness is the implementation of *the* Law, then who but lawyers (until the divinely inspired one returns from hiding) is fit to rule? Shi'ism subdivides into further sub-sects, and according to most, although not all of them, the Imam is in hiding, so that his perfect arbitration and validation are not easily available but remain in reserve, to make themselves available and manifest at some future date. This anticipation of a Second Coming, as well as the strong cult of martyrdom of an Imam, cause Shi'ism to resemble Christianity more closely than do other branches of Islam.

The cult of martyrdom greatly helped the Khomeini movement in its task of mobilizing the masses: Shi'ite scholars are not merely, like Sunni ones, experts on law and theology, but also specialists on the biography of the martyr. Martyrdom is more rousing stuff than jurisprudence and theology, and this enables Shi'a scholars to communicate with the masses more effectively than their Sunni opposite numbers.

Nevertheless, important though the martyrdom theme and the populist potential of Shi'ism were during the build-up to the revolution, this personal element was politically pensioned off by Khomeini once the revolution had succeeded. He profoundly Sunni-fied Shi'ism. In deeply Sunni spirit, he equated Islam with the implementation of *the* Law. The Law was to be enforced neither more nor less severely before or after the eventual return of the Imam. Until such a return, the maintenance and implementation of the Law will be in the hands of the scholars – who else is competent to determine what the Law is? – and in effect, the Shi'ite polity will be a kind of republic with a special bias towards the authority of scholars, a republic implementing the will not of the people but of God, as manifested in a unique Holy Law. Though no doubt welcome, the coming of the Imam will not really make any essential difference to the political situation. So, although the idiosyncrasies of Shi'ism did help it effect the remarkable Iranian revolution, the toppling of a state undefeated in war and with its army and finances wholly intact, none the less the eventual direction taken by the regime is entirely compatible with the general trend from a Low Culture cult of personality to a High Culture reverence for law.

So the Muslim world displays a strong tendency towards the establishment of an *Umma*, an overall community based on the shared faith and the implementation of its law. But what happens to the internal politics of this kind of society? In practice, Muslim polities are pervaded by clientelism. There is government-by-network. The formal institutional arrangements matter far less than do the informal connections of mutual trust based on past personal services, on exchange of protection from above for support from below. Law governs the details of daily life, but not the institutions of power. The entrenched religious constitution of society provides rules for the conduct of life, but no blueprint for the organization of power. This vacuum is filled without protest by clientelist politics. The latest waves of fundamentalists are quite particularly uncompromising in rejection of all institutions which have made compromises with the world. They reign as an absolutely untainted implementation of Islam, and repudiate the old scholars who had made their peace with an impure polity.[2] These latterday puritans have not yet succeeded in seizing power; if they do, it will be interesting to see whether their version of the withering of the (earthly) state will be as catastrophic as the somewhat parallel fundamentalism of the Bolsheviks.

In the traditional world of Islam, Ibn Khaldun had given the classical account of the old form of this system, which continued to be valid for a long time: political order can be based only on cohesion, and cohesion can only be engendered in the rude conditions of tribal life, where no central power keeps the peace, so that a man's security can depend only on mutual trust between himself and fellow members of his camp. In the atomized world of the town, indispensable though it is economically for supplying the needs of society, cohesion was inherently impossible: atomized specialists cannot combine effectively, they are destined for subjugation. Social solidarity and civilized productivity are mutually incompatible: each is found exclusively in one segment of society only. So government had to be the gift of the tribe to the city, renewed every three or four generations or so, when the previous set of tribal conqueror-rulers had become exhausted and had lost its erstwhile unity, its cohesion eroded by urban or civilized life.

Atomization still obtains in what is the modern, much extended urban world, but not much is now left of a tribal womb of political talent. In any case, literal tribes are no longer qualified to fill without further training the complex roles of a modern administrative bureaucracy, and it is rarer for them to defeat a modern army. So, instead, society is ruled by networks, quasi-tribes, alliances forged on the basis of kin, services exchanged, common regional origin, common institutional experience, but still, in general, based on personal trust, well founded or not, rather than on formal relations in a defined bureaucratic structure. The new *asabiyya* is forged on mafia activities rather than on the pasture. The interesting thing about Muslim societies is that this system is not much resented and is widely accepted as normal. What strikes observers is the curious combination of religious moralism and cynical clientelism.

Does this mean that the former is hypocritical? I think not. Rather the reverse. It is as if the society's moral requirements were adequately met by the sheer fact that the state enforces, or at least does not violate, *the* Law; granted this condition, it is accepted that the attribution of positions and advantages should be a matter of rival networks fighting it out, and winner takes, if not all, at least the best of what is going. Not much else seems to be expected of politics. Ibn Khaldun's splendid definition of the state as the institution which prevents injustice other than such as it commits itself, remains valid. The expectation of some additional Civil Society, which could hold the state to account, on top of the *Umma* defined as a shared commitment to the implementation of the Law, would seem almost impious, but in any case unrealistic. The state can be called to account for violation of the divinely ordained Law, or for the failure to implement it, but not for some additional requirements imposed by the popular as opposed to the divine will. In the end, society seems to possess no cement other than the faith on the one hand, and the loyalty, once upon a time of clan and now of clientele, on the other. The residue of the population not locked into any such network is effectively disfranchised: the Law which defines the total community is its sole protection. Its members identify with it rather than with the state, and if the current ruling mafia offends against it too much, they will support a rival network which promises to do better in that respect, and assist its efforts to replace the present lot.

Here then we possess a viable (so far, at any rate) social form, an absolute moral community, which seems to work tolerably in a modern or quasi-modern context, and which accommodates itself without too much discomfort to what are for us political imperfections, provided only that God's will be done, provided *the* Law is respected, even if the state, in Ibn Khaldun's words, assumes and exploits the monopoly of legitimate injustice. Whether or not we like them, the persistence of these societies indicates that they are an option which we must learn to understand, and which constitutes an important variant of the current political condition. If segmentary societies are to be contrasted with Civil Society because the sub-communities on which they depend are too stifling for modern individualism, then Islam provides a further contrast. It exemplifies a social order which seems to lack much capacity to provide political countervailing institutions or associations, which is atomized without much individualism, and operates effectively without intellectual pluralism.

4

THE MARXIST FAILURE

Marxism is now assured of a major, if bizarre, place in world history. For quite some time, it seemed to provide one of the great options available to mankind. At one stage, it looked like the Calvinism of collective and emulative industrialization: the severe but sustained faith which would guide populations through the wilderness, through arduous effort and sacrifices not to be rewarded until much, much later. It also looked like an alternative model which would offer more justice at the price of less liberty. Even if the Marxist crusade failed, it looked as if Marxism would, even with diminished fervour, continue to stand for a rival and alternative sensibility. It was not to be.

It was the first formally secular belief system to have become a world religion and a state ideology in a considerable number of polities, some of them of great importance, and one of them a superpower. There are now far fewer of such polities than there were, and the genuine conviction of the survivors is more than suspect; but for a long time Marxism constituted *the* alternative to liberalism. This being so, its fate is of enormous interest from the viewpoint of determining what can or cannot be done with nominally non-transcendent, this-worldly belief systems.

Of course, the fate of Marxism on its own is not strictly conclusive. The failure of one secular religion cannot absolutely establish, for instance, that secular faiths in general cannot ever be socially effective. Others may yet succeed in the future where Marxism failed. All the same, this is the best and certainly most dramatic and suggestive evidence that we possess so far concerning the issue, and it cannot but profoundly influence our thinking about it. It is worth recapitulating the path which had led to the Marxist alternative.

Generally speaking, human societies maintained order by coercion and superstition. The Enlightenment was right in perceiving this, but deeply misguided in its supposition that it would be possible simply to replace such a system by another, in which society was based on truth and consent instead. There are fairly good reasons why only coercion can constitute the foundation of any social order. Any system in operation must have possible alternatives, both of organization as such and of the distribution of positions in that stable organization. For a very significant proportion of the population these alternatives would always appear preferable, and these people cannot all be assumed to be fools. So it must be presupposed that they would endeavour to bring about that (to them) more favourable alternative, unless restrained by fear. The argument is alas cogent: the rather special conditions which may induce people to accept the social order even without fear, voluntarily, are indeed the pre-conditions of Civil Society, but these do not emerge easily or frequently. Only in conditions of overall growth, when social life is a plus–sum, not a zero–sum game, can a majority have an interest in conforming even without intimidation.

The reason why society must be based on falsehood is equally obvious. Truth is independent of the social order and is at no one's service, and if not impeded will end up by undermining respect for any given authority structure. Only ideas pre-selected or pre-invented and then frozen by ritual and sanctification can be relied upon to sustain a specific organizational set-up. Free inquiry will undermine it. Moreover, theories, as philosophers like to remind us, are under-determined by facts. In other words, reason on its own will not and cannot engender that consensus which underlies social order. The facts of the case, even if unambiguous (which they seldom are), will not engender a shared picture of the situation, let alone shared aims.

Social order requires a shared culture; facts as such cannot, in the nature of the case, engender that shared system of ideas, interpretations and values which make a society viable. Facts are on the one hand recalcitrant, and on the other inadequate.

So, any culture is a systematic prejudgement. Society needs entrenched paradigms. Issues which in the light of reason alone would remain open must be prejudged. No society without culture, no culture without enforced prejudgement. Prejudgement alone makes social life and order possible. To anticipate: our problem is – how could a society emerge in which the prejudgement was made milder and flexible, and yet order was maintained? How was this miracle attained?

Prior to the miracle of Civil Society, human societies habitually lived under coercive and superstitious systems, and generally took such a condition for granted. They were right to do so, there was no alternative. Within such societies, the maintenance of the social order was normally quite properly accorded far more importance than any possible augmentation of the cognitive capital or of productive potential, if indeed those things were valued at all, or held to be attainable or even conceivable. All this was reflected in the values pervading agrarian societies: these values led to a reverence of martial and hieratic skills, a Rule of the Red and the Black. They did not lead to any great respect or encouragement of productive capacity or of intellectual innovation. The specialist was often the object of contempt or fear or both. This, once again, is the normal social condition of mankind. It is foolish to expect anything else.

Then, on one occasion, something rather strange and unusual happened. Certain societies, whose internal organization and ethos shifted away from predation and credulity to production and a measure of intellectual liberty and genuine exploration of nature, became richer and, strangely enough, even more effective militarily than the societies based on and practising the old martial values. Nations of shopkeepers, such as the Dutch and the English, organized in relatively liberal polities, repeatedly beat nations within which martial and ostentatious aristocracies, addicted to the values of aggression and conspicuous display, dominated and set the tone.

'Underdevelopment', though not yet known by that name, was born: societies had come into being, within which the intelligentsia felt there was something basically, structurally wrong and where they believed fundamental reform was possible, desirable and mandatory. They could hardly at that time have been called 'Westernizers', if only because the model which inspired and intrigued them was generally located to the north rather than to the west of them. But the spirit was similar: the *philosophes* of the pre-revolutionary salons were the first Westernizers, or perhaps Northernizers. What had been the normal social condition of man in the traditional world – government by fear and falsehood – was felt to be inherently illegitimate and avoidable. They preached its modification and transformation. Astonishingly, the regime in which oppression and dogmatism prevailed was not merely wicked, but actually weaker than societies which were freer and more tolerant! This was the essence of the Enlightenment. The replacement of fear and falsehood by consent and truth was assiduously held to be feasible. A new social order was to be born under the joint auspices of reason and nature.

When the system which the Enlightenment had been criticizing collapsed in and after 1789, 'enlightened' ideas could be and were tried out. This attempt at implementing the ideas of the Enlightenment did not, however, lead to a rational and consensual order on earth. It led first to the Terror, and then to the Napoleonic dictatorship. A naked actress might impersonate Reason at a revolutionary ritual, but it was not to last: an imperialist and authoritarian monarchy was to be the heir of *the* Revolution.

There had to be a moral in all this, and indeed there was. Human society does not, it would seem, lend itself to the simple application of blueprints worked out in advance by pure thought. That is utopianism. There are constraints inherent in the very nature of the social order, and these constraints must be respected. Social structure has its reasons of which the mind knows nothing. Conservative political thinkers made much of this point, but were inclined to leave it at that, simply issuing an omnibus condemnation of rational reform and interference, and a warning against those who would try to mould society to abstract principles. They eagerly issued an all-purpose *carte blanche* to all political and intellectual malpractices as long as they were time-honoured, on the grounds that they were or might be, at least on balance, socially functional, however absurd or repellent if seen out of context. These as it were indiscriminate conservatives-functionalists are still with us. Starting from the correct premiss that some absurdity and injustice is socially functional, they ignore the fact that some forms of nonsense and oppression are a damn sight less functional than others.

But the conservatives were not the only ones to ponder the lessons of the French Revolution. Some revolutionaries did the same, borrowed a lot from the functionalists-conservatives, who defended the absurdities of the *ancien régime* by crediting them with a hidden usefulness, and came to the conclusion that, though there were indeed constraints operating in history, constraints which would not allow anyone to implement any old blueprint at any old time just like that, nevertheless these constraints were not altogether malign and hostile. They did prevent hasty, facile, ignorant and ill-timed reform, but they might also make even more fundamental change not merely possible but even mandatory and, better still, in the end inevitable. The nature of social and historical reality might be an ally, an expression of progress, and not its enemy. Historical forces were in the end benign. They were not an excuse for ignoring and defying Reason, but rather its secret agents. If properly understood, they were sources of encouragement, support, hope and reassurance. When they were properly understood, as Marx and Engels fondly thought they had indeed managed to do, they showed that the rational order dreamt of by the Enlightenment, based on consent and truth and not on force and fraud, not only *could* come about, but in the end inevitably *would* come about. It was written into the nature of social things that it should be so. Bliss was it in that dawn to be alive.

This optimistic doctrine, which had learnt a lot from the conservative-functionalist doctrine of social constraints and turned these ideas to its own use, was Marxism – perhaps the most elaborate, systematic and best orchestrated of all the attempts to interpret and draw lessons from the French Revolution. It certainly turned out to be the most influential. It came to constitute the major tradition of criticism of the kind of society which was actually emerging in the more advanced parts of Europe in the course of the nineteenth century. It damned not only the past domination of thugs and humbugs, but equally the new domination of entrepreneurs and their ideologists. The apologists of the market appealed to the Hidden Hand, the functionalists-revolutionaries claimed to know the quite different Hidden Hand of institutional camouflage and support of iniquity. Adam Smith's and Edmund Burke's Hidden Hands are quite different. Conservatives invoke both, left revolutionaries claim to de-mystify them. The new vision appealed to all those who disliked the ruthlessness, inequality and inhumanity of the new order. It seemed to offer both a good diagnosis of how that system had come about and of how it functioned, and yet also a good recipe for how it could and would eventually be replaced, and what would replace it. It could claim all at once to be the continuation of its merits – productivity, science – and yet also its abolition and inversion, an implementation of higher values. It would combine the economic growth initiated by individualism with the values of community, and mysteriously combine communalism and freedom.

This doctrine had a quite special appeal in the more backward parts of the world, including the retarded parts of Europe. In such regions, the doctrine promised not merely the rectification of injustice and inequality, but also an overcoming of collective, national backwardness, and hence of weakness and humiliation. With hindsight, it is tempting to say that Marxism was tailor-made for the Russian soul. It enabled it to overcome its obsessional tension between the Westernizing tendency and its mystical, messianic and populist yearnings, a tension avoided by Islam through the availability of its own Higher variant – scripturalist, unitarian and individualist – which promised self-correction without the use of external models.

On the one hand, Marxism claimed to be scientific, indeed to be the very culmination and embodiment of the scientific world-view, and to be its application to man and society; at the same time, however, it castigated the moral compromises of current society, and promised a new order which was totally free and yet also totally fulfilling, devoid of exploitation, inequality and oppression. Within the confines of a single vision, one could satisfy both the messianic longing for a wholly uncorrupted world, a harmonious society, of man at one with himself, *and* the desire to catch up with the Western scientific Joneses. Marxism may even have begun as a message to backward nations – at the time of its first articulation, the Germans – that it is no use trying to catch up, that it was better to join world history at the next and higher stage – and in the end, it became a generalized recipe for catching up.[1]

The religious order, which was set up by the Ignatius Loyola of this movement and which called itself a political party, was committed to the ruthless implementation of the vision. Thanks to favourable circumstances it did manage to seize power and, for a time, not only ruled the society in question, but succeeded to an astonishing extent in persuading it to accept that vision as basically legitimate and morally authoritative. The system ended in quite uniquely dismal failure, above all because, in the end, it simply could not compete technically and economically with the liberal West, and lost both in the arms race and in the consumption race.

When, during an early deep ideological split of the Continent, southern Europe and adjoining areas lagged behind north-western lands, this did not rapidly bring down the regimes linked to the shared backwardness-inducing ideology: the societies could turn in on themselves and isolate themselves, and ignore or live with their economic inferiority, at least for a considerable time. Whether, in the twentieth century, such an option of isolation was really available and might have been practised we shall now never know for certain, but it is doubtful. In any case, such an option was in the end not attempted: faced with unquestionable defeat in the great contest, the leaders of the world's first secular ideocracy decided to open up, and soon found, whether they liked it or not (some did and some were not so sure), that there was no way of stopping or limiting the process, without using methods more drastic than they were by then willing to use – a fastidiousness which is greatly to their credit. One of the new popular sayings of Eastern Europe now is that you cannot be half-pregnant. Everyone knows what it means: you cannot half-liberalize. (As a matter of fact you *can*; but on this occasion it proved impossible to stop the process at some demi-tone of liberty.)

When social orders and faiths crumble there are usually some loyal devotees who fight on in the last ditch. Circular, self-confirming visions cannot be refuted. The true believers always find further confirmation in trials and tribulations. There are always some who have lost their heart to *the* vision, whose psychic need for faith is stronger than their reasons for abandoning it, and who remain loyal in the darkest hour. Not so in the Bolshevik empire: it had no Vendée, and hardly any Bunker. The Bunker it had in 1991 lacked both courage and conviction. Its successors sometimes fought for the spoils and for nationalist reasons, or to retain some of the perks, but virtually no one retained enough zeal or loyalty to struggle for the order and the faith itself. No one, virtually *no one* has a good word to say for Marxism itself. The old *nomenklatura* turned into chauvinists or opportunist-capitalists with impressive and horrifying speed. The countries where they turn to making money are more fortunate than those in which they turn to ethnic cleansing. Never was a sinking ship abandoned with such alacrity and unanimity, never was an experiment condemned so conclusively. Long ago, Machiavelli had said that an Eastern state could be destroyed with one blow, if only it was struck at the centre: here there seems to be the ultimate Eastern state, collapsing through an internally induced softening of the centre, without even a single blow.

When liberalization came and outward adherence to the faith ceased to be obligatory, there was an astonishingly near-universal abandonment of the ideology and a contemptuous indifference to it. Everyone now saw that the emperor was naked. The central intuitions of Marxism – moral, cosmological, sociological – are neither wholly absurd nor wholly without human appeal. Religions in the literal sense have in any case never been greatly vulnerable to mere factual refutation: the harder the faith is to sustain, the more it defines the faithful, the more power it has within the soul, the more it defines identity. It is difficult conditions, such as those which give *offence* to use Kierkegaard's term, which make the believer what he is (and if Kierkegaard were to be believed, nothing else can). The day when prophecy failed was seldom if ever the day when faith was abandoned; rather the reverse. It is also said that faiths do not crumble because they are discredited; they only give way to more attractive rival faiths. But Marxism seems to refute all of this: it was abandoned without any clear or single alternative in sight. People preferred a vacuum to the old creed. They turned to the *zastoi* of liberalism. Why is it that the world's first secular established religion should so patently lack the tenacity, the capacity to thrive on adversity, of its transcendental predecessors? Where did it go wrong?

I doubt whether as yet we possess the evidence required to answer this question. But it is worth looking at the data we do possess, and the explanations which have some plausibility. The obvious fact that Marxism proudly purports to be about this world and not about another one, and hence would seem to be so much more exposed to refutation by the events and facts of this world, does not, I think, explain a great deal. The old religions admittedly claimed to be primarily about another world, but they also said a very great deal about this one, and the falsity of much of what they did say about this world did not trouble them much, if at all. Rather, the authoritative affirmation of falsehood helped to endow them with the special flavour and tension which marks and perhaps defines religion.

What then? A part of the explanation may be sought in the stark, uncompromising collectivism of the Marxist version of salvation, its soteriology. Marxism does promise a total salvation, but not to individuals, only to mankind as a totality. It has virtually nothing to say to an individual in personal anguish or in some kind of life crisis, except perhaps, at most, to advise him to rejoice in the eventual beatitude of all humanity, and to encourage him to help in the struggle and gird his loins for it. A consequence of this was the marked lack of success in creating life-cycle rituals in the Soviet Union, at any rate such as would be linked to the official faith.[2] Marxism has nothing to say to personal tragedy and bereavement.

But there is perhaps an even more important consideration. The great weakness of Marxism may be not so much its formal elimination of the *transcendent* from religion, but its over-sacralization of the *immanent*. It inherited its latent pantheism from its intellectual ancestry, from Spinoza through Hegel. Spinoza had taught that the world was one indivisible unity suffused by the divine, which pervaded it symmetrically. Hegel had added historical movement to this vision, and Marxism was born of this fusion of ideas. It reveres this world and man's activity in it. Pantheism may be a possible state of mind for an unusual, God-intoxicated man such as Spinoza, but it is caviare for the general: the commonality of men require a spiritually stratified world, in which there is not only the sacred but also the profane. Everything may be sacred, but some things must be much more sacred than others. They cannot stand perpetual intoxication with the sacred (even if they like it intermittently), and they need to relax in profanity. It is perhaps this lack of profanity which in the end undid Marxism, which made its hold over the human heart so feeble. It has been said that society cannot make do without the sacred; perhaps it needs the profane at least as much.

By sacralizing all aspects of social life, notably work and the economic sphere, Marxism deprived men of a profane bolthole into which to escape during periods of lukewarmness and diminished zeal. Such periods are inevitable, as there are few individuals, and perhaps no collectivities at all, which can remain indefinitely in a condition of high exaltation. When enthusiasm wanes, it is good to retreat into areas which are neutral, which at least are not in conflict with the requirements of the faith. Routinization is a great boon to faith: without temporary routinization, the perpetual strain and demanding nature of a salvation-bringing faith may be too great. David Hume saw in this the explanation of the puzzle of why Protestant zealots in the end, contrary to logic, were friends rather than enemies of liberty: their universalization of priesthood may have made them ferocious in the days of zeal, but the absence of religious specialists allowed them to be specially lukewarm during the diminution of enthusiasm. Consider Islam: the believer does not abandon the handrail of the faith when he turns to economic activity, in as far as the rules of faith and the obligation to observe them follow him and sustain him. But at the same time economic activity itself is neutral, and its success or failure or its quality do not contaminate the faith.

But in Marxism this is not so. Economic activity has been sacralized, it constitutes both the sacraments and the testing ground for the faith, it is an area in which it would be hard to forget the faith. The icons of this faith depicted the sacredness of work and the worker, astride a tractor seat, muscles bulging with productive effort. Socialist realism was all body, but it was not at all erotic: work not love was being glorified. All this may help explain the striking and interesting fact that massive random terror in the days of Stalin did not undermine belief; rather, it confirmed it. So deep, so tremendous a transformation of the human condition had to be heralded and sanctified in blood; a few feeble trumpets would hardly do. Mass murder did not undermine conviction, but the squalor of the Brezhnev years did have such an effect. When the *nomenklatura* killed each other and accompanied the murderous rampage with blatantly mendacious political theatre, belief survived; but when the *nomenklatura* switched from shooting each other to bribing each other, faith evaporated. The squalor of the work relationship was the equivalent of corrupt priesthood in other faiths.

So perhaps the world's first secular religion failed not

because it deprived man of the transcendent, but because it deprived him of the profane. Marxism claimed to liberate man from religion, from seeing his life through the distorting prism of fantastic notions. By forcing him to endow concrete reality with its full importance and weight, it also made it intolerable. The unification of the political, economic and ideological hierarchies into one single bureaucratic pyramid is not only disastrous for practical performance, it also seems to be catastrophic for the social soul. By sacralizing this world, and above all the most mundane aspects of the world, it deprived men of that necessary contrast between the elevated and the earthy, and of the possibility of an escape into the earthy when the elevated is temporarily in suspended animation. The world cannot bear the burden of so much sacredness. Pantheistic high-minded religions in the past tended to revert, after each attempt to impose 'pure' ideals, to 'corrupt' folk variants which reintroduced the distinction between the sacred and the profane by their idolatry of this or that. Folk Buddhism, for instance, has little resemblance to the elevated philosophical and symmetrical attitude to existence preached by the pure version of the doctrine. But Marxism appears to have no viable vulgar, corrupted folk variant. So perhaps it was its deification of the current and concrete historical process which was its undoing. Mankind seems capable of tolerating Borgias on the papal throne, but not the likes of Brezhnev as archpriests of the sacred revolution which is to liberate mankind and reunite it with its own essence, in unconstrained, fulfilling work. Thugs or humbugs as Mediators with the other world are tolerated, sleazy mediocrities as agents of the Apotheosis of *this* world are not.

So one literally religious *Umma*, the Muslim one, unitarian but retaining the distinction between the divine and the mundane, has succeeded in maintaining its hold over the faithful, and does so with brilliant success; while the other

Umma, articulated in a modern secular and fully monistic idiom, failed dismally to do the same. We have attempted to provide some tentative explanations for both the striking success and the striking failure. Each provides us with part of the context for our attempt to define and understand Civil Society, which differs profoundly from both of them. Whatever Civil Society turns out to be, it is clearly something which is to be contrasted with both successful and unsuccessful *Umma*s, and also with ritual-pervaded cousinly republics, not to mention, of course, outright dictatorships or patrimonial societies.

5

THE SUCCESSFUL *UMMA*

There is a fascinating contradiction in the thinking of David Hume on this topic, a contradiction probably more revealing and illuminating than the consistencies of lesser men. In his *The Natural History of Religion*, Hume works out a sociology of religion which, by implication, at the same time constitutes a theory of the pre-conditions of liberty. His central ideas resemble those of Gibbon and those of that latter-day follower of both Hume and Gibbon, Frazer. They are well in the style and spirit of the Enlightenment, displaying admiration for the virtues of classical antiquity and distaste for the monotheist, scripturalist, intolerant, other-worldly and egotistical ethos which has replaced it.

Classical antiquity inculcated civil duty and social virtues conducive to communal well-being in the real world; Christianity replaced this with an egotistical concern for personal salvation in another world. Hume does not yet have the sophistication of Benjamin Constant or Fustel de Coulanges, and fails to appreciate properly that the liberties of the ancients would not be altogether to the modern taste. The contrast in terms of which he argues is basically one which opposes classical religion – social, civic, this-worldly, communal, traditional, tolerant – to the world religion which replaced it, which on the contrary is egotistic, other-worldly, doctrinal and intolerant. His code word for the former is *superstition*, and for the latter, *enthusiam*, and his conclusions are clear:

> The tolerating spirit of idolaters, both in ancient and modern times, is very obvious to any one . . .
> The intolerance of all religions, which have maintained

the unity of God, is as remarkable as the contrary principle of the polytheists.[1]

The contrast drawn is obvious and the reasoning persuasive. The priests administering the rites of civic religion inculcate social virtues and are not concerned with doctrinal orthodoxy. They barely possess any doctrine as such, or the means for fixing and codifying it. By contrast, the zealots of universal, generic and individually attained salvation through adherence to doctrine, on the one hand encourage their followers to place the salvation of their own private soul above all else, and on the other define membership by adherence to finely specified conviction, deviation from which then defines heresy, and requires punishment. It follows that mankind was much better off under the regime of the ancients, and that the adoption of revealed, doctrinal, scriptural and universalistic religion leads to loss of liberty and social deterioration. The argument is persuasive, and some evidence does indeed support it.

Yet something is not quite right. Even in *The Natural History of Religion*, which in the main is devoted to expounding the Augustan theme of the excellence of the ancients and the corruption of the moderns, Hume comments on the counter-example:

> . . . if, among Christians, the English and the Dutch have embraced principles of toleration, this singularity has proceeded from the steady resolution of the civil magistrate, in opposition to the continued efforts of priests and bigots.[2]

The greater liberty of the English and the Dutch clearly contradicts the Augustan thesis, and Hume invokes the questionably adequate *Hilfshypothese* of the civil magistrate and his steady resolution, so as to overcome the difficulty.

This won't really do, and elsewhere Hume does rather

better. His remarkable essay, 'Of Superstition and Enthusiasm', deserves to be counted as one of the earliest and most perceptive contributions to the debate concerning the role of protestantism in the emergence of the modern world. In it he puts forward three propositions:

> . . . superstition is favourable to priestly power, and enthusiasm not less, but more contrary to it, than sound reason and philosophy.
>
> Religions which partake of enthusiasm are, on their first rite, more furious and violent than those which partake of superstition; but in a little time become more gentle and moderate.
>
> . . . superstition is an enemy to civil liberty, and enthusiasm a friend to it.[3]

Here we are no longer in the pre-Fustel world of Gibbon which equates the good social condition with the best that is to be found in antiquity, but rather in the world of Max Weber, pervaded by the awareness that something very distinctive has happened in the modern world and that it is connected with the Reformation. Contrary to the earlier argument, enthusiasm is a friend to liberty after all! Individualist, doctrine-centred, serious faith, which abolishes priesthood by turning every man into his own priest, and lays upon him the burden of his own surveillance and the perpetual and intense anxiety this brings in its train – strangely but indubitably, all this is the ally of freedom! The initial model had clearly entailed the contrary; but the facts of the case now point in the other direction.

The last of the three propositions sums it all up; the other two offer attempts at explanation of this strange phenomenon, so contrary to the plausible reasoning of *The Natural History* cited earlier. The explanation offered is close to what Max Weber was later to call 'routinization': the religions addicted to 'enthusiasm', i.e. to firm commitment to abstract doctrine and its serious implementation, though initially uncompromising and to that extent inimical to liberty, eventually soften and become tolerant.

They make a double (at least) contribution to freedom: first they destroy the priests, in part by universalizing priesthood and thus terminating the existence of a distinct priestly caste, and secondly, they become directly favourable to liberty during the period of diminution of zeal. This diminution is aided by the absence among these erstwhile enthusiasts of a special category of people charged with maintaining the flame of faith. That very equalization of the religious condition, which had made the puritans such zealots and formidable enemies of liberty at the time of maximum fervour, by enlisting *all* men in religious hysteria, also made them more tolerant during the time of diminution of enthusiasm . . .

All this is excellent, and immeasurably superior to Hume's other attempt at explaining the liberal potential of enthusiasm in *The Natural History*. But the balance of power in society, as between the enthusiasts and the addicts of superstition, must surely also be taken into consideration. Might not the full story run something like this? The enthusiasts made great inroads on the society, and in fact were for a time victorious. None the less, in the end they were defeated, though not crushed. The society as a whole favoured a compromise, a partial retention of superstition, priestly power, ritual and all, though with limited power, *and* moreover combined with a toleration of the extremists-enthusiasts, who, obliged to renounce their ambition of imposing righteousness on earth if necessary by military and political force, turn instead to pacifism and tolerance. Their efforts to impose righteousness on earth are defeated, but they are not so crushed as to be prevented from practising righteousness within their own moral ghetto, and demanding with success toleration for their excessive but private zeal.

Unable to ensure that the will of God be done on earth as it is in heaven, they turn inward, impose it on themselves, and in the outer world turn towards productive activity as much as to religious zeal. Or rather, they turn to economic activity, practising it with religious zeal and disinterestedness. Only such Platonic, pure, disinterested acquisitiveness could engender that work ethic and sustained accumulation which produces a modern economy. Those who merely pursue worldly goods for wordly ends would not plough back their profits and thereby initiate the miracle of economic growth: only puritan entrepreneurs do that. Virtue not greed finds the path to true affluence. Greed but not virtue engenders free riders who undermine trust and so pervert the economy. Their abstention from further political ambition also made the puritans acceptable to the power-holders, for they are no danger to them, or at any rate are no longer such, and so they need not be and are not segregated in a social ghetto like earlier pariah capitalists. The old rulers can marry rather than confiscate the new wealth, an altogether more amiable arrangement, and one which aids the general commercialization of society. This option is all the more attractive if the old land- and honour-oriented ruling class practises primogeniture, so that its younger sons are not averse to acquiring wealth by other means, such as marriage or even work.

So the coming of Civil Society, a society liberal in the modern sense, rather than the ancient, non-liberal cousinly and ritualized plural and balanced society, presupposed a political stalemate between practitioners of superstition and the zealots of enthusiasm, such as in fact did occur in seventeenth-century England, leading to a compromise. This allowed a diminished, sliding-scale ritualism and mediation at the centre, and a privatized *Umma* at home, among the minoritarian enthusiasts who turn to the economy rather than a *jihad*.

But many times over, this routinization and compromise were not open to those secular Calvinists, the Bolsheviks. For one thing, they could not be seduced into compromise and routinization because they were politically too successful. In this they resembled the Muslims. They had won their Civil War. Moreover, their utterly monistic, unitarian crypto-theology (going back ultimately to Spinoza, through Hegel) sacralized the world, all the world, far too much. For the old puritans, work, successful work, was merely the sign of election, but not its essence. For the Marxists, work was human salvation itself. At the same time, subjecting it to the polity, they could not leave it alone. When, through political centralization, it became sordid, it could not offer an escape, available during a period of reduced enthusiasm. Managers who dribbled their way between the threat of punishment for failing to fulfil the plan, and punishment for violating legality (which was the only way to fulfil the plan), could hardly develop a work ethic. They developed a mafioso intrigue ethic, which they carried on into the post-Communist world, where they learnt to speak *laissez-faire* rather than Marxese. Those who (like the present writer) were once, long ago, tempted to see Marxism as the Calvinism of collective and emulative industrialization altogether missed the point: Calvinism could have the effects with which Weber credited it by partially sacralizing work in a profane world governed by political compromise. It could not have done so in a politically *un*compromising world from which profanity had been banned, and in which there was no bolthole for routinized enthusiasts.

6

A CONTRAST BETWEEN THE
ABRAHAMIC FAITHS

When doctrinal, soteriological, omnibus world religions partially replaced communal, ritualistic, specific religions in the 'Axial Age', they seldom if ever replaced them completely. The doctrinal, individualist, universalist element was introduced as a great revelation. The doctrine or illumination of total salvation was offered to any questing individual; this was added to the community-defining ritual and guardian priesthood surviving from the past. Henceforth, the religious life of mankind in more complex societies was due to be the interaction of these two major elements, sometimes fusing harmoniously, sometimes in overt confrontation. The manner in which these two elements met in Christianity and in Islam is interesting: the two cases are virtually mirror images of each other.

In Islam, the scripturalist, puritan, universalist, individualist variant prevailed at the centre. Not always endowed with political power, it was nevertheless ascribed normative authority. It set the tone, it identified and authorized what were recognized as the highest values. The ritualistic, mediation-addicted, ecstasy-given, hierarchical variants were fragmented, peripheral, popular and often a little shamefaced. So: *Umma* at the centre, local community at the periphery, and religious emulation of community in the lower levels of the social hierarchy. Central authority was mainly linked to the first religious style, and local communities to the second.

Periodically, conflict erupts between the two: the enthusiasts at the centre for a time prevail over the superstition at the margins, but social factors eventually restore the balance.

50

In Europe, the contrast between community and society is one between the past and the present: we move from community to society. In Islam, these two were ever present, synchronic: community at the margins, society at the centre.

Come the modern world however – imposed by extraneous forces rather than produced endogenously – and the new balance of power, favouring the urban centre against rural communities, causes the central faith to prevail, and we are left with a successful *Umma* at long last. This is the mystery of the secularization-resistant nature of Islam discussed above.

In Western Christianity the mix of the two religious elements was quite other. Hierarchy, organized mediation, bureaucratized ritual and magic prevailed in the central single organization, claiming a monopolistic link to the Founder of the faith and source of the unique revelation. The scripturalist, puritan, individualistic, symmetrical, ecstasy-spurning and mediation-repudiating enthusiasts were at the margin. They were disunited, whereas the organization was unique and united (at least most of the time, when not undergoing temporary schism).

It was this mix which engendered by some strange internal chemistry the modern world. Whether only it could have done so, as a very great sociologist seemed to suggest, we shall probably never know: we cannot re-run the experiment in order to find out. This mix, plus the fact that the great confrontation between superstitious centre and enthusiastic periphery ended in a draw and in some places in deadlock, eventually meant that the modern world was produced. When it emerged, in the end the compromise led not to a general *Umma*, nor even to a series of ghettos, but to a widespread secularization. And also, and this is what concerns us in the present argument, it eventually led to a Civil Society, to a pluralism free not only of the imposition of the *Umma*, but also of the cousinly ritualism of communities.

By now we have at least four situations to consider: the pluralist but stifling 'segmentary' communities of pre-Axial days; the Muslim *Umma* which succeeded eventually in establishing itself, though ironically only under the impact of defeat by an alien expansionist industrial civilization; the Christian marginal *Umma* which failed, but in so doing engendered Civil Society; and the would-be secular Marxist *Umma* of the immanentist, this-worldly, socio-historical religion, which clearly failed as an *Umma*, and has not as yet demonstrated its capacity to produce a successor Civil Society either. All it has achieved so far is to generate, at least among a significant proportion of its erstwhile citizens, an evidently sincere and ardent desire for Civil Society – but that is hardly the same thing.

One should perhaps also consider further social options: pre-industrial centralized empires, 'patrimonial' states, generally superimposed on subjugated local segmentary communities; and successful emulative industrial societies, which have borrowed industrial-scientific techniques (sometimes with outstanding success) but not, or not altogether, the elements of industrial society which had first engendered the society of sustained productive growth.

7

CIVIL SOCIETY COMPLETES THE CIRCLE

There is a certain fittingness in the notion of Civil Society becoming the central slogan in the dismantling of Marxist society because, as stated at the beginning, the central intuition of Marxism can be summed up as the claim that Civil Society is a fraud. Its partnership with the state was a fraud, or so it was claimed: they were in collusion, the state was a covert agent of a dominant sub-part of Civil Society, and not at all a neutral peace-keeper and arbitrator. It only presented itself as such. The moral community of Civil Society was itself equally fraudulent: it masked the pathological institutionalization of greed and acquisitiveness, alien to real human nature, in a game in which victors and vanquished alike were both victims in the end.

It turned out that it was after all the alleged Marxist overcoming of the idea of Civil Society which was really fraudulent. The alleged fraud in fact contained something enormously valuable and indispensable. In the end, it was not that the expropriators were expropriated, but rather that the would-be de-mystifiers were shown to be the greatest perpetrators of mystification and fraud.

I am not suggesting that those Soviets and East Europeans who turned to this notion in the course of the 1970s and the 1980s did so deliberately, consciously enjoying the irony of turning the tables on the faith which had wrecked their lives. Whereas the reformers of the Soviet world in the 1950s still wished to invoke Marxist ideals and slogans, those of the 1980s were sick and tired of Marxism, and far too contemptuously indifferent to it even to bother to score such points. They no longer paid it the compliment of rational opposition, to use Jane Austen's phrase. I doubt whether they were greatly concerned or even conscious of this aspect of the matter: rather, they turned to the phrase because it did convey, in a concise and very suggestive manner, precisely that which they most lacked and most desired. The aspiration for Civil Society was born of the social condition of Eastern Europe and the Soviet world.

In the hands of these critics of the Bolshevik social order, the content of the notion is luminous and simple: the end of the monolith, of the monopoly of the political and social organization, of the monopoly of truth and information, all of which characterized 'really existing socialism'. That phrase was coined in one of the last attempts by the system to justify itself: it was meant to tell romantic far-left critics that they had better not expect too much, be content with the kind of socialism which was to be found on earth and refrain from harping on its faults.

As we have stressed, all this tacitly presupposed that the pluralism which would replace centralism would be a pluralism of a special and desirable kind, different from the pluralism of segmentary societies, ancient or tribal, which, though not tyrannical in a centralized kind of way, is nevertheless stifling. This was not a problem uppermost in their minds, or indeed present at all: though a Solzhenitsyn may think of a return to the simplicities of north-east rural Russia, a return to some long-lost Slav tribalism is on the whole not on the agenda. Within the Russian right there is actually a small strand which wishes to locate the Slav soul not in the Orthodox Church, but in pre-Christian paganism: the Conversion of Vladimir was presumably the very first Zionist plot against Holy Russia. But though the historical reconstructions of Slavonic paganism are interesting, it is not politically important. Archaeo-populism is not a significant strand in contemporary Eastern Europe, and those who speak of Civil Society have no need to spell out that they are not reviving pre-Christian Slav clans.

Although the notion of Civil Society is indeed simple, the historical concept to which it is linked is tangled and elusive. Given its roots partly in Hegelo-Marxist metaphysics – a tradition whose authors can hardly be held up as models of lucidity – this is perhaps not too surprising. Their prose and thought were indeed, to use John Maynard Keynes's word, 'turbid'. So, if the link with this pre-history of the concept is to be established, a little tidying up is necessary.

First of all, what exactly was it that Civil Society was being compared and contrasted with in that tradition? A contrast is crucial at two quite different levels, and the thinkers of this tradition do not always make this distinction clear. On the one hand, there is the contrast between societies within which a realm other than the political claims to exist, and those where it does not. In feudal society, as political and economic strata are conspicuously visible and manifest, indeed are legally and ritually underwritten, it would seem everything is clear. There is no pretence. There is also no separation. There is only one social order, political and economic. There is no talk of Civil Society as distinct from the state: there is only overlapping, identical political hierarchy and economic specialization, mutually reinforcing each other. Political rank and economic function are firmly welded, and one entails the other. The political subject is also the peasant, the owner of the land is also the ruler and judge. Political and economic specializations are linked to each other.

What is contrasted is a society in which there are two quite distinct realms, the political (which is also moral) and the socio-economic (which is morally neutral and instrumental). In as far as there is no deception in societies of the feudal kind, which appear to wear their structure on their sleeves, is one to say that there is no social pathology among them? This doesn't sound quite right. *Less* of it? Is it, like temperature, to be measured in degrees? One can hardly do the metaphysics of a system one does not believe in, but one must record one's puzzlement. Something does not seem to have been thought out to the end. Marxism wobbled somewhat between a condemnation of capitalism alone, and a condemnation of all class-endowed societies, and there was a logical strain between the implied premisses of the two repudiations.

Having contrasted societies containing this separation and those which do not, we are also concerned with the internal contrast within the former type. This is Civil Society in the narrower sense: that part of society which stands opposed to the political structure (in the context of a social order in which this separation has taken place and is possible).

One must concern oneself with this internal confrontation. An interesting question here is – in what sense precisely is it that Civil Society is fraudulent? Is it because it really *is* that which it pretends to be, or because it *is not*? It pretends to be the area of individual self-interest and free pursuit of private ends: is it this brazen egotism which makes it bad? But if so, where is the deception? Is the fraudulence then to be found not in Civil Society as such but in the total social structure, in the pairing of Civil Society and its protector-state, in the spurious neutrality of the latter? Or is it Civil Society on its own which is already morally spurious, since its formal egalitarianism does not make visible the hidden inequality, the loading of the social dice, the real powerlessness of the formally free, and all the secret agendas, the separation of the owners of capital from the others and their tacit collusion with the state? Both these themes seem to have been present, but their mutual compatibility is less than obvious.

Marxist doctrine seems to hold that each of these two partners is fraudulent on its own, and also fraudulent in their partnership. Civil Society, atomized productive individualism based on private property, is not really required, in the

Marxist view, for the carrying out of the productive business of society. On the contrary, without class division engendered by the un-symmetrical relationship to the means of production, men would spontaneously organize themselves and attend to the 'administration of things' without, it would seem, having to rule each other. Part of the doctrine appears to be, however, that this is possible only at a high level of productive forces, and also for some reason at a very low one, at the very beginning of history – but not in the intervening stage of moderate, not very high level of productivity, which constitutes the Marxist version of the Fall, between the Garden of Eden and the Second Coming. But it also seems to be part of the doctrine that the Fall was functional and necessary for the economic development of mankind: the Fall not only provided the redeemers with a task and a justification, it also gave them – and *only it* could give them – the tools for the job . . .

At the same time, the state is also redundant because the coercive management of conflict, far from being inherent in the human condition as such, is only required in the condition of the presence of antagonistic classes, acutely present but hidden (in the main by the fraud-state) in the fraudulent-Civil-Society. In the social order in which it is present in its most acute form, class division is marked by the myth of a neutral benevolent state and by the formal but unreal egalitarianism of Civil Society.

The picture I have been drawing is heavily indebted to a remarkable essay by Leszek Kolakowski, 'The Myth of Human Self-Identity: Unity of Civil and Political Society in Socialist Thought'.[1] The author has the great advantage of being both an authoritative historian of Marxist thought and a person who has lived through the entire cycle of faith and disillusionment in Eastern Europe. I have however used my own words and it may well be that I have failed to do justice to Kolakowski's intentions and meaning.

The interesting aim of Kolakowski's essay was to trace the parallelism between the weaknesses of the original Marxist critique of the notion of Civil Society, and the historic weaknesses of the societies emerging from the attempt to implement Marxist ideas. While stressing the fact that reality is always more complex than ideology, he notes that:

> . . . an ideology is always weaker than the social forces which happen to be its vehicle and try to carry its values.[2]

Kolakowski goes on to show how the misguided aspiration of the theory has a marked convergence with the appalling defects of societies practising 'real socialism', societies which at the time he was writing were still rather more numerous than they are now.

The underlying moral aspiration which he credits to Marxism is the abolition of the separation between the social and the political. (This would seem to be the tacit unacknowledged romantic thread in Marxist thought and sensibility – which damns capitalism but, by implication, absolves the social order which preceded it, with its fusion of political and economic hierarchy, notwithstanding its class-endowed, oppressive and exploitative character.) It is this which troubles society, and it is this which causes the deep ache within the human heart. It is this which has deprived us of our human unity, externally in the social order, and internally in our souls:

> The dream of a perfectly unified human community is probably as old as human thought about society . . . it has strong roots in the awareness of a split which humanity has suffered apparently from the very beginning of its existence after leaving animal innocence . . .[3]

Kolakowski goes on to say that, given the actual constraints of human nature (conflict does not arise only from class opposition) and of industrial organization, the attempt to implement this re-unification of the soul and society can only end in the kind of tyranny which has in fact pervasively, and without any exception, characterized Communism. This is entirely convincing, and time has given it proof – though it could profitably have been said more clearly without all these socio-metaphysics. As he then puts it more eloquently:

> . . . there is no reason to expect that this dream can ever come true except in the cruel form of despotism; and despotism is a desperate simulation of paradise.[4]

All the same, even as an exposition, it does not altogether add up. The alienation in the soul etc. is now said to be co-extensive with the very history of humanity, having begun at the point of departure from animal innocence. What happens to primitive Communism on this interpretation? Were only the primates free of alienation? Or, if the cruel separation of the social and the political is so particularly characteristic of bourgeois society – with its formally equal citizenship in the supposedly moral state, conjoined with its brutal inequalities in the amoral market – why should we not, as indeed many romantics have, look back with nostalgia and sad longings at feudal society, in which, *ex hypothesi*, the social and political were co-extensive and neither needed to hide its face? Now *there* was a social order which did not fear to speak its name . . . There seems to be a terrible vacillation about the dating of the departure from the Garden of Eden: was it at the end of 'animal innocence', or at the departure from primitive Communism, or at the end of the feudal order? It would seem important to date the Fall firmly . . .

These and similar obscurities quickly spring up as soon as one tries to make too much sense of the notion of Civil Society and its role within the tradition in which Marxism was articulated. It is all a little bit too abstruse to be equated with something which has aroused political passions among broad East European masses. Did men really take great risks and make sacrifices, seized by a passionate desire to abolish the distinction between the social and the political within their own souls? It doesn't sound quite convincing. Men do not rush into the streets under the sway of quite such complex and ambiguous metaphysical sentiments. At least, I should not have thought so. Were they really struggling against this seductive yearning in their own hearts, in the end, when they turned violently against the society spawned by Marxism?

The currently operational notion of Civil Society is useful, and not quite so tortuous. It did not acquire its recent popularity and potency for nothing. But giving it a down-to-earth sociological meaning – institutional pluralism *of a certain kind* – is more useful than turning back to the turgid ideological tradition from which it sprang. Its muddles, even in the hands of a brilliant expositor such as Leszek Kolakowski, in the end stray beyond the bounds of sense. The notion does need to be endowed with more than one contrast and to be given a realistic historical context. We need to see it against the backcloth of multiple historical options for our social world is a complex place. We need to go beyond the simple binary opposition of pluralism and Bolshevik Caesaro-Papism, for the options of our world are not exhausted by this contrast. But in doing so, I fear we get little help from the muddy obscurities of the Hegelo-Marxist tradition.

8

ADAM FERGUSON

Historically, Adam Ferguson's *An Essay on the History of Civil Society*[1] is one of the points of origin of the use of the expression Civil Society. However, Ferguson's work is of far more than merely historical interest. His manner of handling the problem, which clearly haunted him deeply, helps to throw light on the contemporary issue connected with this notion, notwithstanding the fact (or perhaps all the more) that the situation he was facing was quite different from the one prevailing now, over two centuries later.

Like his contemporaries of the Scottish and Continental Enlightenment, Ferguson was an observer of the transition from aristocratic to commercial society, and of a society, though he was not properly aware of it, destined to become industrial. Ferguson was not an economist. In his book he disclaims, rather convincingly, expertise in this field, referring to it as 'a subject with which I am not much conversant', and refers the reader to a work which is soon to appear on the subject, by one Mr Smith, author of the *Theory of Moral Sentiments*. Ferguson's direct observations on economics do indeed seem muddled and unsure. But when it comes to the social and political implications of economics or economic sociology, his perceptions are profound and important.

Ferguson anticipates and perhaps partly shares in a curious error of Adam Smith, who attributed the switch from feudal-aristocratic independence to the fact that the nobles allowed themselves to be seduced by 'baubles', as Smith was soon to put it, by the temptations of conspicuous display through possession of prestige objects, by switching their expenditure to the acquisition of such objects, rather than the recruitment and maintenance of retainers. Here Smith confused cause and effect: in an effectively centralized state, a tail of retainers ceases to be of much use, indeed their deployment is prohibited, while baubles constitute a more liquid and storable, as well as a more acceptable and effective, form of wealth and display. Ferguson notes the same tendency, but places it in the context of centralized, monarchical government: 'The Sovereign himself owes great part of his authority to . . . the dazzling equipage which he exhibits in public. The subordinate ranks lay claim to importance by a like exhibition, and for that purpose carry in every instant . . . the ornaments of their fortune.'[2] This seems to be closer to getting the causal connection right, though there is still a suspicion that display on its own may be credited with a greater political role than it really possessed. Still, it is interesting that the 'theatre state' was present and noted in the West, and is not an oriental speciality. If the notoriously middle-class Hanoverians could be seen in this light, what should be said of the Bourbons, Romanovs and Habsburgs?

What, however, really distinguishes Ferguson is that he is a bemused, perplexed and rather worried observer of the kind of Civil Society which he sees emerging. He understands full well what distinguishes the society emerging in Europe in his time from earlier societies, including those of classical antiquity. His account of the difference is very similar to the one which Emile Durkheim was due to offer a century later, using the expressions Mechanical and Organic Solidarity.[3] Like Durkheim, Ferguson focuses on the social division of labour.

'By having separated the arts of the clothier and the tanner, we are the better supplied with shoes and with cloth.'[4] Nothing very contentious here, and Mr Smith was due very soon to bestow great notoriety on this idea. But Ferguson immediately proceeds to the heart of the matter, the point at which the division of labour really acquires crucial implications for society. The next sentences read: 'But to separate the arts which form the citizen and the statesmen, the arts of policy and war, is an attempt to dismember the human character, and to destroy those very arts which we mean to improve. By this separation, we in effect deprive a free people of what is necessary for their safety; or we prepare a defence against invasion from abroad, which gives a prospect of usurpation, and threatens the establishment of military government at home.'[5] Like Durkheim, he sees that the socio-political consequences of the division of labour are even more important than the economic ones.

The thought continues to haunt him: 'The boasted refinements, then, of the polished age, are not divested of danger. They open a door, perhaps, to disaster, as wide and accessible as any of those they have shut. If they build walls and ramparts, they enervate the minds of those who are placed to defend them . . . they reduct the military spirit of entire nations . . . they prepare for mankind the government of force.'[6]

This is at the heart of Ferguson's anxiety. Civil Society is all very well in itself, but by separating the rulers/warriors from the civilians, the arts of the citizen from those of war, does it not create the danger of a take-over by the former, which will destroy the benign order which had itself engendered the separation? *That* is the danger!

Ferguson's contemporary Gibbon had noted with a touch of incredulous surprise that the barbarians had gone, or at any rate had been greatly reduced in relative numbers and strength, so that the danger which had in the end overwhelmed ancient civilization was no longer present. The nobles of Poland, Germany and France can stand up to whatever the Asian steppe can throw at them. Ferguson does not think that this particular danger menaces Europe either: on the contrary, he notes the new disproportion of strength between Europe and the rest, and perceptively anticipates the consequence, namely the emergence of the colonial empires which in fact were the fruits of that disproportion in the nineteenth century.

It is not the external danger which troubles him, it is the

internal consequences of the diminished participation in coercion by a population of a 'polished' society, whose citizens turn to production rather than martial honour, and allow legitimate coercion to be not just a specialism but a monopolistic specialism of a single institution, the state – a point which a later theorist, Max Weber, was to turn into the very definition of the state. This surely must be a danger, Ferguson nervously insists.

Here Ferguson unwittingly echoes the theorist of another civilization, Ibn Khaldun, who made the same point, not at all as a nervous anticipation, but as a simple matter of fact: producers who delegate security to others, to specialists of government and war, become politically and militarily emasculated and helpless.[7] Specialists–producers cannot but do this, in Ibn Khaldun's world, for their specialisms atomize them and preclude that cohesion which is the condition of political and military effectiveness. So urban specialists simply had no choice. Only *un*specialized producers can be real citizen-soldiers. In the world which Ibn Khaldun knew, this was indeed true, and for this very reason there was and could be no Civil Society in any real sense. Specialized, atomized producers were politically helpless victims of cohesive, unspecialized tribesmen, who manned the citadel and in effect constituted the state. In the world familiar to Ferguson this was not true, it had not happened yet. Something rather like it nearly happened in 1745, but significantly the enterprise failed. Consequently Ferguson's warnings have more the tone of an uneasy disquiet, rather than a confident prediction of disaster – though he does use that word, as we have seen. He refers to Demosthenes often, and half, but only half, assumes his posture . . .

A Demosthenes was not called for in eighteenth-century Europe, though Ferguson flirted with such a posture. The danger was not really that concern with productive and commercial activity would turn the minds of citizens away from civic virtue to such an extent that they would no longer be longer be able to resist an external menace, or succumb to internal coercive specialists whom they had called in to ward off external dangers. Ferguson was not really in a position to understand what the real new dangers would be: the new society had not by then revealed itself sufficiently to make such a discernment possible. But his reflections on dangers which were no longer real illuminate the social order with which he was concerned.

He also has his half-optimistic moments, when he rejects the suggestion that men must choose between (politically participant) virtue and (politically supine) concern with wealth. He does indeed speculate that those who 'think of nothing but the numbers and wealth of a people' do so 'possibly from an opinion that the virtues of men are secure', whereas those who 'think of nothing but how to preserve the national virtues' do so 'from a dread of corruption'.[8] But the optimist within him repudiates the fork: 'Human society has great obligations to both. They are opposed to one another only by mistake . . .' It would seem that we might have both modern wealth and ancient virtue, or at any rate not be wholly bereft of either, and enjoy a society based on both virtue and affluence. So, if we are lucky, we may enjoy both participation and wealth! Ferguson does not anticipate a new Civil Society in which a participating liberty is actually based on wealth . . .

In opposition to anyone who tried to impose an uncompromising dilemma between affluence and virtue, Ferguson observes quite correctly that 'the characters of the warlike and the commercial are variously combined: they are formed in different degrees by the influence of circumstances . . .'[9] But at other times, as we have seen, he is not too sure of his guarded optimism, and it is this anxiety and vacillation which inspire his excellent and profound reflections.

The Romans are praised for their lack of specialization, in other words freedom from indulgence in the division of labour, even in the matter of martial skills. '. . . the antagonists of Pyrrhus and of Hannibal were . . . still in need of instruction in the first rudiments of their trade'. But instruction they took, even if it had to be from gladiators. '. . . the haughty Roman . . . knew the advantage of order and union, without having been broke to the inferior arts of the mercenary soldier; and had the courage to face the enemies of his country, without having practised the use of his weapon under the fear of being whipped'.[10] But Ferguson goes on to say that the Roman

> . . . could ill be persuaded, that a time might come, when refined and intelligent nations would make the art of war to consist in a few technical forms; that citizens and soldiers might come to be distinguished as much as women and men; that the citizen would become possessed of a property which he would not be able, or required, to defend.[11]

Ferguson clearly credits the Romans with an aversion to specialization, and a pride in amateurism, a feeling which the English also liked to indulge later, notably in contrast to humourless Prussian professionalism. Ferguson evidently feels that the Romans had a point: he who allows the specialist to take over a crucial aspect of life is giving hostages to fortune.

A more contemporary example Ferguson uses is that of an American (redskin) chief addressing the (British) governor of Jamaica at the beginning of hostilities with Spain. The chieftain was astonished not only by the smallness of the body of armed men at the disposal of the governor (who was waiting for reinforcements from Europe), but even more by the presence of civilian, merchant spectators, who were not being enlisted for the conflict. The governor explained to him that the merchants and other inhabitants took no part in the service. The chief was appalled at this idea of such civilian status. '. . . when I go to war, I leave nobody at home but the women . . .'. The chieftain was clearly voicing the natural sentiments of a participatory society. Here Ferguson assumes a superior air and comments that this 'simple warrior' evidently could not realize that among us in sophisticated nations, war and commerce were not so very distinct, that 'mighty armies may be put in motion from behind the counter, . . . and . . . how often the prince, the nobles, and the statesmen, in many a polished nation, might . . . be considered as merchants'.[12] The fact that war is carried on by specialists in a sense also makes it commensurate with other activities: it is a continuation of commerce by other means, or perhaps the other way round. Ferguson does not patronize the Romans, but he does patronize the redskin.

However, Ferguson does not always take this air of *hautain* superiority.

In the progress of arts and of policy, the members of every state are divided into classes; and . . . there is no distinction more serious than that of the warrior and the pacific inhabitant; no more is required to place men in the relation of master and slave. Even when the rigours of an established slavery abate, as they have done in modern Europe . . . this distinction serves still to separate the noble from the base . . . It was certainly never foreseen by mankind, that in the pursuit of refinement, they were to reverse this order; or even that they were to place the government, and the military force of nations, in different hands. But is it equally unforeseen that the former order may again take place? and that the pacific citizen . . . must one day bow to the person to whom he has entrusted the sword? If such a revolution should actually follow, will this new master revive in his own order the spirit of the noble and the free? . . . I am afraid to reply.[13]

What he is perceptively saying is that the emergence of Civil Society was unprecedented and had 'certainly never been foreseen by mankind'. It does indeed go against the normal, natural order of things. His concern is: could it not be reversed again?[14]

He does not adequately analyse the distinctive conditions which have led in modern north-west Europe to the subordination of coercers to producers. He does not, as Karl Marx was to do later, elaborate a theory of the subjection of coercion to production (let alone commit the Marxist absurdity of generalizing this idea for all of human history). Ferguson clearly is afraid of the prospect of a return of the old priorities, and refers to the absence of Bruti and Fabii, once the praetorian bands became the Republic in Rome. Coercion might return in praetorian rather than pristine civic form: that is his fear.

Yet Ferguson also has his sanguine (though still anxious) mood. If binary thinking – wealth or virtue – is a mistake as he hopes, it is something which nevertheless haunts him. He is far from completely sure that it is a mistake; he likes to think it is, but can't help wondering . . . As it happens, it is indeed a mistake. But it was not a silly anxiety, and Jakob Burckhardt was to echo it in the next century on the basis of a more extensive experience of modern European society.[15]

Ferguson's basic model is one involving the interaction of honour and interest: commercial societies replace martial ones, and while he is not unpleased about the process, he is anxious concerning its permanence or irreversibility. To put it simply, he fears a backlash of honour, and of a rather inferior kind – the domination of praetorians rather than the self-government of a free and proud people.

One weakness or deficiency in Ferguson's account is that, while describing the interplay of the main two participants, he does not consider the role of religion. In that respect he is inferior, for instance, to David Hume. Ferguson's main account of the emergence of the modern state is simple: the monarch in alliance with the people subdues the feudal lordships, freeing the people from subjection to the lords, and encouraging the practice of commercial and lucrative arts. This could sometimes strengthen the crown, but it could also turn against it and lead to 'a spectacle new in the history of mankind; monarchy mixed with republic, and extensive territory, governed, during some ages, without military force'.[16] This is the favourable, British variant of the story. Nothing in all this about the possible role of the Reformation . . .

Nevertheless, there is one area where Ferguson does accord a place to religion of a kind, in the genesis of the social forms with which he is concerned. History is not only the interaction and competition of honour and interest: on occasion a third partner, virtue, also enters the stage. A society committed to the imposition of virtue is different from one either addicted to honour or seduced by interest. In its uncompromising devotion to virtue, and its ruthless subjection of its citizens to its practice, it is indeed an *Umma*, a charismatic community, of a kind.

Ferguson, however, is not thinking either of the Muslims or of the Puritans: what he has in mind is Sparta. He quotes Xenophon: '. . . the Spartans should excel every nation, being the only state in which virtue is studied as the object of government'.[17] Making virtue the prime object of government is indeed a good definition of an *Umma* or of a charismatic community. Ferguson calls the Spartans a singular people, in that 'they alone, in the language of Xenophon, made virtue an object of state'.[18]

A devotion to virtue so complete does indeed make the society a kind of sacramental community. But this one single intrusion of religion into Ferguson's scheme does not really modify it: all that religion achieves in this case is to

strengthen beyond all normal measure these political attitudes which are otherwise sustained by honour alone. The
excess leads only to a quite exceptional rejection of comfort
and interest and diminishes, as no doubt it was intended to
do, the danger of seduction by luxury or by greed. In
Sparta, devotion to honour becomes so extreme as to constitute a form of virtue. But this is not relevant to modern
concerns. Modern society is not tempted by a return to
segmentary tribalism nor, *a fortiori*, to a virtue-obsessed
form of it. It only encounters this social option in the form
of charismatic sub-communities such as the kibbutzim. These
are indeed (or were) Spartan, ascetic and virtue-oriented, but
they appeal only to ideologically very committed minorities.
In the modern world, it is very hard to diffuse such a spirit
throughout the whole of a society, or to preserve it for
long. Virtue-oriented, self-selected sub-communities are exceedingly prone to routinization.

So all in all, Ferguson was worried about a danger which
in the end did not arise, at any rate in the form he envisaged,
and to that extent he misread the world he inhabited. But if
we ask ourselves what it was that Ferguson perceived in the
current situation and considered to be a problem, we shall
see more clearly what it is that really characterizes Civil
Society, and what its problems are.

Societies are concerned with the maintenance of order
and survival in the face of enemies on the one hand, and
with the maintenance or enhancement of production on the
other. The two concerns dominate societies in various proportions, but by and large one could say that, almost by
definition, the first concern predominates in 'rude' societies,
and the second in 'polished' ones. The first concern can be
satisfied in two ways: by centralized power (tyranny), or by
some kind of participation. The latter naturally requires
from those who take part in it a manly spirit, and a
willingness and capacity to defend oneself against oppres-

sion. As Montesquieu put it, republics are based on the virtues of men, and tyrannies on their vices. The values which encourage this kind of attitude may be summed up as 'honour'.

By contrast, the values which constitute the orientation towards production, commerce and comfort may be termed 'interest'. Ferguson notes a strong tendency towards a shift from honour to interest in modern European nations. In itself, this makes the world richer and more populous, and there is nothing objectionable in it. But here is the rub: this enhancement of production and life's comforts depends on the division of labour. Nothing wrong with this either, when it simply involves the separation of the clothier's and the cobbler's activities, indeed of their persons. But the matter becomes graver when it also separates the citizen from the warrior and the statesman: to put it in the simplest terms, may not the market lead to a new serfdom? Long before Hayek expressed the view that the abolition of the market would constitute a 'Road to Serfdom', Ferguson feared the very opposite: the market itself, and not its elimination, would lead that way.

Ibn Khaldun had brilliantly analysed a world in which precisely this had indeed happened, where commercial specialists were politically helpless in the face of a state based on cohesive unspecialized tribesmen, though Ferguson was unaware of this. Ibn Khaldun accepted a world in which civility and cohesion were mutually incompatible, and where the ensuing problem was solved by the *cities* providing the first element, and *tribes* the other. The situation was stable, except for a certain cyclical movement within it, which however left the overall pattern unchanged. Ferguson faced an unstable society in which there was a marked shift towards civility, and he feared that the resulting imbalance could lead to subjugation.

Ferguson was wrong, altogether wrong: what he feared

did not happen. Warriors have not taken over advanced commercial-industrial nations. Even when a curious coalition of warriors and industrialists tried this on in inter-war Germany and Japan, they were eventually eliminated. Military rule characterizes unsuccessful rather than successful interest-oriented nations: it is not the division of labour, but a relatively low level of it, which leads in that direction. We know that now. But the reasons which made him think what he did were good ones, and by looking into why they did not in fact operate in the real world we shall learn a good deal.

In other types of society, the kind of situation which Ferguson observed in modern Europe did in fact in the end have precisely the kind of consequences which he feared. Commercial populations, which relied on others for their politics and/or defence, were liable in the end to lose their internal or external independence, or both. Of the commercial city republics of early modern Italy, only Venice survived into the eighteenth century, and then only as a shadow of its former self – and it too fell without resistance at the mere approach of Napoleon. Machiavelli, separated in time from Ibn Khaldun by only a few generations, saw the same problem in a more difficult and less stable environment, and offered a similar but more pessimistic diagnosis. In Machiavelli's world, only the Swiss in his view still exemplified ancient honour, but could hardly be expected to provide the rest of Europe or even Italy with rulers. They only supplied transient mercenaries, and not even Mamelukes (mercenaries with tenure), while, in the world of Ibn Khaldun, Turks, Arabs and Berbers provided an inexhaustible supply of cohesive rulers/warriors, capable of complementing the uncohesive atomized specialists of the productive urbanized and sedentarized world. Flaubert's *Salammbô*, a curious work using a society which has cause to fear its mercenaries, is used as a parable for a society terrified by its own hired workers.

Participatory self-government is a sturdy plant when it grows among pastoral or mountain peasant communities, and many such have survived well into the modern world; but when combined with commercialism, the plant is seldom long-lived, though liable to have a splendid flowering. Commercial city states are a fragile rather than a hardy plant. Why should the free merchants of north-west Europe fare any better than their predecessors who lie buried in the historic past?

There are some good reasons why this fate did not befall them (though these reasons escaped Ferguson):

1) Perpetual and exponential growth. What happened in eighteenth-century Europe was not merely one of those revolutions, which may have occurred on previous occasions, in which commerce and production for a time take over from predation and domination as central social themes and values. This had indeed happened before, and then the resulting political instability made it short-lived; but this time it was accompanied by two other processes – the incipient Industrial Revolution, leading to an entirely new method of production, and the Scientific Revolution, due to ensure an unending supply of innovation and an apparently unending exponential increase in productive powers. This meant that the new social system was in the end endowed with an unlimited Social Bribery Fund. It could eventually bribe its way out of any external or internal threat. In any case, its technological superiority dispensed it from the need to pay any Danegeld to barbarian outsiders. The Gatling gun could see to that.

2) Civil Society could achieve this, and *only* it could do so; and Europe was a multi-state system. This is important, for although the new social order could acquire the means to pay off discontent, it could only do so if it was left in peace to operate the new economy. There was no guarantee that the specialists in politics and coercion whom it used would necessarily allow it to operate in peace and undis-

turbed: in their greed, they might well kill the golden-egg-laying goose. Ferguson's fears were not altogether unjustified. In fact, on at least two very important occasions, they did precisely this: the agents of the Counter-Reformation and the Bolsheviks each throttled a large part (not quite the same part, though they overlap) of Europe. Coercers and ideologues took over from producers or dominated them, with disastrous consequences. But in a plural state system, in which other states prosper dramatically and visibly, the throttling and throttled systems are in the end eliminated by a social variant of natural selection. In a multi-state system, it was possible to throttle Civil Society in some places, but not in all of them: and the civil societies which did survive then demonstrated their economic, and even military, superiority over the authorization polities which spurned interest, and sought only honour or virtue, or some unsavoury combination of the two. The Red and the Black even sustained each other. A multi-state system helped ensure that Civil Society, which restrains its Reds and Blacks, survived in some places at least, even if throttled elsewhere. The economic and even military superiority of a growing society then eventually obliged the others to follow suit. Natural selection secured what rational foresight or restraint had failed to bring about.[19]

3) In these circumstances, within the un-throttled societies production becomes a better path to wealth than domination. In traditional societies, he who has political power soon acquires wealth as a kind of consequence. This is not altogether unknown even in commercial and industrial societies, but it is incomparably less important. There, the best way to make money is to make money. It is quite possible to do this without acquiring or bothering too much with power. (This virtually defines Civil Society.) The economy is where the action is, and it is possible to indulge in economic activity without attending too much or even at all to

problems of power. Not all industrialists have retinues of thugs, nor are all of them mafiosi and not all of them bribe bureaucrats. Not all of them have friends at court. It is possible to prosper while simply attending to one's business. This is another way of saying that the law protects wealth, independently of whether one has formed special alliances or groups of followers for its protection. Wealth leads to power, more than the other way around. This is both remarkable and exceptional. Marxism made it into a reproach when it should be a source of pride, and it absurdly generalized the dominance of production over an alleged political 'super-structure' as a law governing all class-endowed societies, when in fact it is a unique characteristic of one type of society.

4) The division of labour assumes a completely new form. It is not merely that there is far more specialization than there had been before: it is a qualitatively different kind of specialization. Ferguson saw some of this: he saw that what really mattered was not merely the separation of the clothier and the cobbler, but the separation of the citizen and the soldier. But there is more to it than just separation: it is the *manner* in which they are separated which has changed, and this is supremely important. This is something which escaped even Durkheim a century later, when he lumped together diverse kinds of complex, 'organic' divisions of labour, without really distinguishing with adequate emphasis the difference between a complex advanced traditional civilization and the modern industrial world.

In one sense, the division of labour has now gone further in industrial society than ever before: there are more distinct and separate jobs. But in another sense, there is less of it and there is far more homogeneity: every job is carried out in the same style and in much the same spirit. The manuals and the rules are articulated in a publicly shared and accessible idiom, for there is mobility between jobs, retraining is relatively easy, and guild monopolies rare; a generic education fitting a man for all the specialisms is more important for his identity than the specific training which fits him for his particular job. Occupational mobility is the norm. Also, specialisms are inter-locking, specialists are obliged to communicate with and understand other specialists, they have to 'speak the same language'.

In other words, men are primarily members of a shared High Culture (i.e. of a nation), and only secondarily, if at all, members of a guild or caste. In consequence, though the separation of the military from other functions, which Ferguson feared as the harbinger of a new and worse rule of praetorian thugs, does indeed occur, in another sense the military specialism is made to resemble all others: it generates no caste or estate, it is a profession like any other, like agriculture for that matter. Movement into it and out of it is not restricted, and its remuneration follows the laws of the market rather than the law of extortion, which had in the past enabled those who could coerce to take as much as they wanted from those who could not. Modern societies have farmers not peasants: agriculture is an occupation like any other, which can be both entered and left without crossing legally or ritually sanctified borders of an estate or a caste. It has soldiers but not a warrior caste. The same holds true of politics and the profession of arms: the Black and the Red are not legally or sacramentally distinguished from the rest of society. Off duty they generally dress in civilian garb. You can hardly tell them apart. The commander of the highly successful British expedition to the Falklands took pride in the fact that he was a commuter-to-a-job. He was not a military aristocrat or a member of a warrior caste.

It is this unique kind of division of labour which explains that strange feature of Civil Society – exceedingly strange in a comparative historical context – namely, that those in positions of power are not remunerated out of all proportion

to all others (nor committed to some excess of ascetic virtue)
but, on the contrary, that their rewards are relatively feeble
and nothing much out of the ordinary. In traditional society,
this could only occur in those very participatory communities which ensured the temporary nature of occupancy of
powerful positions – for instance, by selecting the holders by
lot, as did the Greeks, and for a limited time only – or
which, as in the Spartan case which so impressed Ferguson,
made a fetish of ascetic virtue and imposed it with special
emphasis on its own leaders.

5) Self-policing or modularity. A type of religion emerged
in Europe with the Reformation which eschewed external
sanctions and the ritual underscoring of social obligations,
and, on the contrary, laid on each individual the enormous
burden of being his own priest and internal judge. Whether
this ethos engendered or followed an economy increasingly
oriented towards individualism is a much discussed question.
Such a disinterested and individually sanctioned pursuit of
virtue clearly made a significant contribution to the emergence of Civil Society: according to Tocqueville, it is this
which made democracy viable in America. Virtue as the aim
of state or public policy is probably disastrous for liberty.
Virtue, freely practised between consenting adults, may be a
great boon to Civil Society, or even its essential pre-condition. Concern with virtue led men to a disinterested pursuit
of interest – accumulation without enjoyment, hence to re-
investment, hence continuous growth – rather than transformation of wealth into power, status, pleasure or salvation, as
is more common among men. It was disinterested interest
which lay at the basis of capitalism, according to Max
Weber; and it was individually chosen rather than socially
enforced vocation which produced a mobile and innovative
society. Ironically, it was men who took their vocations
very seriously who produced a social order in which vocations became optional. There is no general Social Contract

for all societies, only specific types of Fundamental Law for each kind of society: and individual commitment to contract not status seems to be a foundation of this social order.

6) The ideological stalemate. For virtue to be privatized, what may be essential is that the practitioners and preachers of uncompromising, absolute and enforced virtue, and the practitioners of the old rival, socially rooted and socially adaptive ritualistic religion should terminate their conflict in stalemate, and so in mutual toleration, as happened in England. This encourages the ritualistic traditionalists to provide the overall social framework, but to do it with a light hand: their rivals after all are not unbelievers, but rather those who believe with excessive conviction and sincerity. The Anglican Church was more concerned with combating the enthusiasm of the Puritans than with infidelity. It also leads the Puritans to turn inwards, and incidentally to disinterested and hence most effective accumulation, and indeed to preach and practise tolerance, as they need it for themselves. The disinterestedness of their pursuit of wealth is not only most beneficial economically, it is also most beneficial politically. As they do not use their wealth for the acquisition of power (any more than they use it to purchase either pleasure or salvation, as had been the usual practice of mankind), they break through the vicious circle which in the past obliged power-holders to suppress successful accumulators of wealth, as an imminent political menace. They can be tolerated, as they themselves no longer seek power.

7) Political stalemate (made possible by growth). This is something of which Ferguson is fully aware, though he fails to link it to the ideological stalemate. The political stalemate generates that blend of monarchy and republic which he admired in England and which led to a unique perfection of the rule of law.

In his remarkable *People, Cities and Wealth*[20] E.A. Wrigley points out that the great classical economists, normally held to be the prophets of emerging capitalism, were in fact exceedingly nervous, not to say pessimistic, about its prospects. They saw internal economic contradictions within it which would eventually lead it into trouble (views taken over in modified form by their disciple Karl Marx). Ferguson should be counted alongside them, as a person preoccupied not with economic contradictions (which he did not claim to understand), but with its political contradictions, which he sensed acutely. The interesting thing is that both kinds of pessimism came to be invalidated by the same factor, by the tremendous expansion of productive power consequent on the impact of scientific technology. The victory of commercial over predatory society in the eighteenth century was for once made permanent and stable, and did not in the end destroy itself, because the commercial revolution and the political one were in due course complemented by the industrial-scientific one, which supplied the means by which it could make itself permanent and secure. In somewhat the same way, the emulative modernization of Islam led to a permanent victory of High Islam over Folk Islam, whereas in the past these could only oscillate in a kind of cyclical pattern.

We have considered, in reverse historical order, two deep reflections on Civil Society: Leszek Kolakowski's account of what troubled the Marxist tradition concerning Civil Society and Adam Ferguson's as it were anticipatory concern with its political viability. The two forms of anguish are exceedingly different in style and human tone. The Marxist one belongs squarely to the world of nineteenth-century romanticism. Its tone is that of the *Sorrows of Young Werther*. Man wants to be whole, and complains bitterly that he finds his soul bifurcated between political and economic concerns. Marxism, it would seem, wanted a man free of the separation of the economic and selfish man from the political and moral one: unity of soul was the underlying idea. The earthy realism of the eighteenth-century Scot does not leave room for such recherché anxiety: he is less bothered about what the division does to the soul than about what it may do to society, the danger that it may lead to a disagreeable form of servitude.

In fact, this separation is an inherent feature of Civil Society, and indeed one of its main glories. The price of liberty may once have been eternal vigilance: the splendid thing about Civil Society is that even the absent-minded, or those preoccupied with their private concerns or for any other reason ill-suited to the exercise of eternal and intimidating vigilance, can look forward to enjoying their liberty. Civil Society bestows liberty even on the non-vigilant.

Only the brave deserve the fair, says the poet. But may we not aspire to a social order in which even those of us who are timid can enjoy feminine beauty? Such has always been my pious hope. Civil Society is an order in which liberty, not to mention female pulchritude, is available even to the timorous, non-vigilant and absent-minded.

9

EAST IS EAST AND WEST IS WEST

The relative geographic distribution of social atomization is interesting. At any rate, there is a striking difference on this point between two thinkers, Machiavelli and Tocqueville.

In a remarkable passage (and one which has earned him denigration as an ancestor of modern 'Orientalism', in the pejorative sense of Orient-basher), Machiavelli contrasts the problems and difficulties of conquest in Western and Eastern societies. Nothing is easier, he suggests, than the beginnings of an invasion of a Western kingdom: given its fragmentation into autonomous or independent feudal sub-units, it is easy to find an ally among the discontented barons and, with his aid, enter the realm. And one can add that it is not even all that difficult, with the help of such local allies, to win a victory over the local monarch and displace him. It is then that the real difficulties begin. The fragmentation which had made initial entry so easy makes effective and unchallenged domination difficult or impossible.

How different it all is in the East! One faces a united absolutist kingdom, and to defeat such a powerful enemy with so good a military base may indeed be difficult. But if, like Alexander, you succeed in securing a decisive victory, thereafter all is easy. The society had been politically and militarily pulverized, and once the central force is destroyed, nothing else remains. After one crucial victory, domination is easy, unchallenged and permanent.

Tocqueville, over four centuries later, was also an analyst of Western society and an acute observer of the East. His own involvement in French politics led him, in the period of the July Monarchy which was also the beginning of French implantation in North Africa, to become much concerned with Algeria. The central theme of his reflections is exactly the opposite of the Florentine's.

Discussing the war with Amir Abd el Kader, originally a rural marabout who had built up an Algerian state in opposition to the French on the ruins left behind by the departed Turks, he makes an observation which is diametrically opposed to Machiavelli's. As far as the Turkish overlords were concerned, he might indeed have simply echoed Machiavelli: one single decisive battle destroyed the Turkish principality based on Algiers. The defeated Ottomans offered their services to the new victors and when the offer was declined could be packed off into an astonishingly small number of boats and sent off to Istambul. Their rule was indeed based on the concentration of force in one place and the fragmentation of the rest of society. They ruled a segmented Algerian society with an astonishingly small number of men, as the French noted with bitterness when at the end of their own period in Algeria *they* in turn required 400,000 men for the same task.

When the French originally came up against local resistance the story was entirely different. Tocqueville stresses precisely that in the struggle with Abd el Kader, who was in effect the leader of all the tribes actively hostile to the French, but whom the Kabyles, for instance, refused to support, it was quite useless to hope for or even seek a decisive encounter, or to suppose that there was some central point whose capture would decide the outcome of the war. The French were facing a society which did indeed crumble into dust in defeat, but could reassemble as quickly as soon as conditions were favourable.

Both Machiavelli and Tocqueville were perceptive observers, and the Near East had not changed so very radically between the early sixteenth and nineteenth centuries. Under the surface domination of the Ottomans, the world of Ibn Khaldun lived on. So which of the two men was right?

The answer is of course that both were. They had focused on different aspects of the East. The Eastern central state did indeed have the properties Machiavelli credited to it: it was not the apex of a complex pyramid of power, within which, in fact and in law, there was a dispersal of effective authority. A single victory over a unique power centre did indeed render the rest of society helpless in the hands of the victor. But by no means all of the East, and in particular not the arid parts of the Middle East, were effectively governed from some such urban or unique courtly nerve centre.

The local political theory might indeed be absolutist, but reality was different. A great deal of the countryside, in particular when difficult of access owing to mountainous relief or desert, was populated by self-governing, auton-omous or independent social units. These were exceedingly difficult either to conquer or, if conquered, to administer. They could easily splinter in defeat and flight, but as quickly reassemble into a formidable force under a leader endowed with the fragile charisma of success. No exemplary court dominated society. A strong centre might be paramount, and it might control vulnerable, urban and sedentary areas, but much of society was partially or totally autonomous, in actual practice negotiating and re-negotiating its relationship with the centre in the light of an unstable balance of power.

Such communities had become relatively rare in Europe, even by the fifteenth or sixteenth centuries. Machiavelli, who knew that they had once been common, indeed consti-tuting a kind of norm in antiquity, noted that in his Europe only the Swiss lived like the ancients (i.e. displayed powerful cohesion sanctified by seriously observed religion). In North Africa and many parts of the Middle East, those communities had survived long enough to play an important political role well into the twentieth century. Iranian and Moroccan tribes played a significant role even when the formal idiom, though not the reality, of politics had moved towards the emulation of Western phraseology. There were, at least nominally, constitutionalist or even socialist tribes . . .

Machiavelli faced the same political problem as Ibn Khaldun, his predecessor by a couple of generations or so, and the same problem which was to worry Adam Ferguson so much later, at a time when it had ceased to be acute: what was to be the realistic basis of social order, who were to be the defenders of the state, satisfying the old and difficult Platonic requirement of behaving as valiant sheepdogs against external wolves, but not behaving like wolves themselves towards the sheep under their care? A very difficult question. Civic armies drawn from urban populations did not amount to much, while mercenaries would take over if successful, and desert if liable to be defeated. Machiavelli was perplexed by the problem and had no very good answer, other than recommending the use of mixed forces, presumably in the hope that they would not all run away or attack you at the same time. It was the best he could think of, and it was not a terribly impressive solution.

Ibn Khaldun was better off when it came to solutions for the same problem. He didn't even have to invent the solution for himself: the society he studied and which surrounded him had provided the solution many times, quite regularly, and it seemed to work. The extensive social backwoods of savannah and mountain provided an enormous reservoir, a kind of political womb of cohesive communities, well able and indeed obliged to defend and to administer themselves: these could also run a larger state when given the chance by the decline of a previous dynasty (which had itself emerged in a similar fashion). The state was a gift of the tribe to the city.

Ibn Khaldun did not even bother to commend this solution. He simply analysed the process as a matter of fact, as the only possible social order, a law of social functioning. It was validated by its inevitability, more than by its relatively beneficial effects. In any case there is no point in deliberating over what could not be otherwise, as Aristotle observed.

Machiavelli could not adapt that solution to Italy and Europe. Only the Swiss had the required ancient virtues, but there weren't enough Swiss to go round, and in any case, however formidable as soldiers (the French, Machiavelli noted, could not win either without them or against them), they simply do not seem to possess the imagination and panache required for state-building in foreign parts. The Normans had indeed once done this from one end of Europe to the other, from Dublin to Palermo and Kiev, but the Switzers seem to lack that certain political *savoir faire*. So?

What is important is that the problem Machiavelli could not solve, and which Ibn Khaldun solved so to speak from stock, from the actual current practice of his own society, was about to be solved in Europe in an entirely new way in the course of the centuries which separated Ibn Khaldun and Machiavelli from Ferguson and Tocqueville. In the West it was not the question of an option, as it once had been in classical antiquity, between participant community and centralized empire: the pluralist semi-segmentary feudal state had already been replaced by the modern state, first baroque and monarchic and then participatory and 'democratic'. Tocqueville stressed that the Jacobin republic merely continued and completed the centralizing work of the French monarchy, or one can equally say that the centralizing monarchy with its respect for property had already prepared the ground for the Civil Society which the modern democratic state completed. The so-called absolute monarchy was not all that absolute: it respected law and property. Even the most absolutist of European monarchies, the Russian, deeply impressed a nineteenth-century visitor from Persia by the extent to which power-holders were subject to law.[1] (Severe oppression of the peasantry was the obverse of respect for the rights of the gentry, a service aristocracy whose loyalty was bought by the security of its property and privileges. It was only the much later Bolshevik abolition of property rights and re-imposition of serfdom which subjected both the service *nomenklatura* and the re-enserfed peasantry to equal arbitrariness.) This was the baroque state's most significant feature, as Perry Anderson stressed in *The Lineages of the Absolute State.*[2] In its shadow, an independent Civil Society emerged, not supine, ready in due course to take the state to account and able to do so.

This was the mystery: here there was an effective central state which, while acquiring such great power, nevertheless did not pulverize the rest of society, rendering it supine and helpless. A society emerged which ceased to be segmentary – either as an alternative to the state, as a mode of efficient statelessness, or as an internal opposition to the state or in part its ally – and yet was capable of providing a countervailing force to the state. All the logic of past social forms militated against the mere possibility of such a phenomenon, but all the same it did emerge. That is the mystery of Civil Society.

POLITICAL CENTRALIZATION AND
ECONOMIC DECENTRALIZATION

There are two main reasons why economic decentralization is essential in industrial society and certainly constitutes a pre-condition of anything resembling a Civil Society.

Such a society can only be plural – and contain countervailing forces and balance mechanisms, which are located in the economic sphere or work by means of economic power – precisely because effective political-coercive centralization is a necessary pre-condition of its functioning; hence there cannot be much balancing in the coercive sphere. Traditional societies can and sometimes do have pluralism in the sphere of order-maintenance. As economic and social structures are not separate from political ones, they must have it in that joint sphere if they are to have it anywhere at all.

In as far as such political pluralism presupposes eventual or occasional violent conflict, the units which oppose each other and which from time to time enter into conflict must have a hold over the loyalty of their members, sufficient to induce them to fight and to risk loss of life. In consequence, as already stressed, they are heavily ritualized.

In modern industrial society, this profound aura attaches only to the total community, the national state, and perhaps to the preservation of its basic political order. It does not attach to sub-units, which are optional and superficial. A man is not expected to die for his county or borough or his office community. He is not obliged to wear clothes indicating his membership, and he is not even obliged to support the local football team. He can without inviting insult or injury support a rival team. There are clubs of Inter Milan supporters outside Milan, or of Manchester United supporters outside Manchester, and their members are not excluded from the rites and social life of their local communities – they can attend their local garden fête with impunity. That might have been difficult in the ancient city, but is acceptable in the modern one. A man can change links of that kind without shame or stigma. What George Santayana said about our nationality and our relations to women – they cannot be changed honourably, and they are too accidental to be worth changing – does indeed apply to country, but no longer to county. You can change your county without formalities, ritual, trauma or treason. This was not so in days of clans and lineages. The total national community is still very significant – or rather, it is more significant than it has ever been before – but its sub-units have lost their potency.

For these various reasons, political pluralism in terms of independent or autonomous coercive units is *out*. Local units simply lack the adequate weight. Liberty, on the other hand, is impossible without pluralism, without a balance of power. As it cannot be political, it must be economic. (Ideological pluralism is yet to be discussed; for the moment, the argument assumes two options only.)

The second argument for the indispensability of economic pluralism – i.e. the existence of genuinely independent productive and property-controlling units in society – is the argument from economic efficiency, from the pre-conditions of economic growth (which in turn is almost certainly a pre-condition of the kind of social pluralism we want).

Political hierarchies obey the law which probably governs most human societies – namely, that from the viewpoint of any sub-unit in the hierarchy (whether it be an individual or a group), the maintenance of the position of that sub-unit must be the primary and dominant consideration, trumping by far any concern with the efficient performance of the task formally assigned to it.

The notorious inefficiency of Communist economies, finally made so manifest in the disclosure of social accounts in 1989, springs primarily from this source. The best commentary on Communist economies is Václav Havel's story about the Czech beer-brewing enthusiast, who − beer being the heart of Czech life − devoted his entire energy to improving the quality of the output of the brewery in which he was employed.[1] In the end, he was sacked with ignominy as a saboteur. Innovation and efficiency are inherently disruptive.

Does it follow that the proper way of running an industrial society is on the night-watchman state principle, with the central coercive authority looking after defence and order only, leaving all else to the 'market'? This does not follow, nor is it remotely true. The 'market' model of Civil Society may be applicable to the very special conditions prevailing in eighteenth-century Britain, in the course of the first emergence of industrial society. Those conditions included the existence of, above all, a fairly feeble technology, one just about capable of improving significantly on traditional methods of production, and making sustained innovation appear attractive, but not capable of very much more. A feeble technology of such a kind can be given its head and it will not disrupt either the social order or the environment, or at any rate not too much. Compare this with the technology available at present: any unrestricted use of it would − and quite possibly will − lead to a total disruption of the environment and the social order. The indirect consequences of modern technology are terrifying. Moreover, technical innovation is often on a very large scale and irreversible. In brief, both its scale and its consequences are such that they cannot but concern society as a whole: it is no longer a matter of temporarily blackening the odd Lancashire dale.

There is also the moral legitimacy and acceptability of an

uncontrolled market to consider. Technical innovation at the beginning or in the course of the first Industrial Revolution was not too far removed in its ideas from the shared common sense of the society. The inventors of the time were mainly practical men of good sense, not abstract scientists at the very boundaries of current scientific theory. The rewards accruing to innovation consequently had a kind of legitimacy: they were the recompense of innovative enterprise on the part of those so rewarded. These men really brought benefits to their society.

Today, innovation is the fruit of an overall scientific advance, and the actual inventor is only the fortunate last link in a long chain to which countless others have contributed. In fact, notoriously, it very often is not the inventor of the new idea who is rewarded by its implementation. Disaggregation of the actual contribution to the advance is almost impossible. Rewards are random, and frequently go not to creative innovators but to those well placed to be insider traders. Economic activity takes place in a social, not a natural environment: successful operators are not victors over nature, but smart-alecks who know how to steal a march in the intricate corridors of the economic machine. The legitimacy of such wealth is far from persuasive.

There is another moral aspect of all this. The mobility of modern society has led to the existence of small social units, notably the nuclear family, and moreover one in which both adults are employed. The recent sexual revolution has frequently made the social unit even smaller. Such small units in which adults are generally in full employment simply cannot shoulder the burden of looking after those who are, one way or another, disabled. In what is basically a very affluent society, the existence of widespread destitution among the handicapped and isolated members of society is morally repellent. A modern society without some form of effective welfare state is unutterably repulsive.

There is also the bulky, package-deal quality of the provision of services, and of the control of the environmental effects of a modern style of production and consumption. In modern societies, something approaching half the national income passes through the hands of political authorities. It is inevitable that this should be so, even if defence spending should eventually decline. The infrastructure is large and lumpy, and it can only be erected and maintained by the collectivity.

But the fact that so much of the economic demand is inevitably under the control of political agencies of one kind or another is that we are not dealing with a genuinely neutral market situation, in which demand is determined by the interaction of individual tastes and the natural environment. The modern entrepreneur mediates between a politically controlled environment and society, rather than between nature and society. Formally, modern societies try to legislate against 'insider trading', the economic use of information concerning the political creation or determination of an environment which has ceased to be natural, and has become social, politically created. But in fact, it is of the very essence of a modern economy that it is based on insider trading. There is no other kind. There simply is no 'outside' with which to trade. When the methods of production need to adjust themselves for optional effectiveness, not to nature, but to a socially created and politically variable manipulated environment, information about and contact with that crucial political milieu is what makes the difference between success and failure. The night-watchman who controls more than half the environment cannot be a neutral servant. Modern corporations snap up senior civil servants and politicians who opt for early retirement, not because they are genuinely impressed by their intellectual equipment – they are not – but because their inside knowledge, their ability to know just who it is in the state machine who needs to be rung up for any given end, is invaluable.

The lumpiness and irreversibility of major decisions, the enormous size of the socially maintained infrastructure, the inevitability of insider dealings and the importance of insider information jointly ensure that the pure-market-cum-minimalist-state model bears little relation to what actually happens or to what is either remotely possible or desirable. The most effective modern economies are those which practise a loose state–economy co-operation, working on the basis of informal networks and pressures, without depriving productive units of their autonomy and liberty of movement, but frankly recognizing the significance of the state as weather-maker, and the inevitably political nature of major economic decisions.

IDEOLOGICAL PLURALISM AND
LIBERAL DOUBLETHINK,
OR THE END OF THE ENLIGHTENMENT ILLUSION

The simplest formula for Civil Society, then, is political-coercive centralization with accountability, rotation and fairly low rewards for those manning the political apparatus, and economic pluralism. Maintenance of order is not delegated to sub-units, but concentrated in the hand of one agency or co-ordinated cluster of agencies. The economic pluralism however (reinforced by both the reality and the anticipation of growth) puts limits on political centralism, compelling it to remain within the bounds of its prescribed and restricted role. What of the third sphere of human activity, ideology? Should it resemble the political sphere in its centralization, or the economic one in its pluralism?

The best way to approach this is perhaps by way of a discussion of the great illusion, or delusion, of the Enlightenment. The Enlightenment was concerned with describing, and above all denouncing, the society it was rejecting and which it hoped was passing for ever – a society based on tyranny and superstition. The rule of kings and priests was to give way to the rule of Reason and Nature. If falsehood had endorsed, legitimated and underwritten oppression and exploitation, would not a luminous truth engender a new, free and happy social order? It seemed a plausible hope, and the *philosophes* were dedicated to its propagation.

Reality does not seem so simple. The implementation of Reason in the event led first to the Terror and then to the Napoleonic dictatorship. What had gone wrong? The nineteenth century pondered the question, and the most celebrated and influential answer ran: ah, we had neglected the laws of history and society.

This was the lesson which Marxism claimed to have learnt. It possessed a plausible theory of the evolution of that social material, and of the conditions which would eventually make it ready and receptive to the formation of a rational, free social order. So this sociologically more sophisticated, improved version of the Enlightenment, you might say the Enlightenment Mark II programme, was also applied, at first with appalling faith and confidence, and lo and behold: it also led to a tyranny, an incomparably worse one, and incidentally it also led to inefficiency and squalor far worse than anything ever engendered by the first version, by the original Enlightenment naïvety. After seventy years, the experiment collapsed in a uniquely ignominious manner, unrivalled in history. Past tyrannies and superstitions had their loyalists and true believers; but when Communism crumbled, initially no one raised a hand in its defence. Its adherents turned to economic opportunism or to chauvinism and may have regretted their lost stability, but as for their faith, they shed it without any inner struggle. Never was a total faith relinquished with such ease.

The reality of the matter seems to be that, whereas a traditional tyrannical order was indeed liable to be based on conviction which was both strong and mistaken, a free order is based in the end not on true and firm conviction, but on doubt, compromise and doublethink. There are various reasons for this. For one thing, either laws of social development are not there to be found, or at any rate no one has found them. Secondly, the superior kind of truth available in science is both unstable and largely lacking in any clear social implications. Its links with the world of daily life, the 'lived world', the *Lebenswelt*, are wobbly. The *Lebenswelt* now needs to be given a name, precisely because it no longer exhausts the world, it is no longer *the* world, and can no longer be taken for granted. It is an interim compromise. As Lewis Wolpert correctly pointed out, if anything is part of 'common sense', i.e. built into the assumptions of daily life, it is almost certainly false.

The world in which men think seriously, and to which serious thought refers, is no longer identical with the world in which one lives one's daily life. The instability, contestability and often incomprehensibility of the serious, respectworthy kind of cognition, and hence of its objects, make it and them altogether unsuitable to be the foundation of a stable, reliable social order, or to constitute the milieu of life. The mechanisms underlying that cognitive and technological-economic growth on which modern society depends for its legitimacy, require pluralism among cognitive explorers as well as among producers, and it is consequently incompatible with any imposition of a social consensus. The attempt to impose it, in Marxist societies, in the end proved catastrophic, and helped bring about their eventual disintegration.

But the old imperatives of social life still apply: men must still live in the same world and share the same concepts at least up to a point, and society must still have its rituals or at least a few of them. So? The answer is that the common conceptual world sustained by shared ritual still does exist, but its authority is greatly diminished. Attendance at rituals is optional, experimentation with concepts tolerated. The shared world could no longer be taken with the utmost seriousness. It is provisional, good enough as a kind of daily shorthand, but suspended when serious issues are faced. That too is of the essence of Civil Society. Daily life is sacralized at most in an ironic spirit.

George Orwell invented the term 'doublethink', a kind of parody of the term 'dialectic', to designate the manner in which members of the faith-committed new tyranny combined emphatic adherence to dogma, not only externally but also internally, while knowing full well at another level that what they were affirming was rubbish. He meant it to characterize the typical and inescapable mental condition of the new ideocracy.

But in fact, doublethink also characterizes the new liberalism. It was born of diminished conviction, of a failed *Umma*, of a compromise between the believers and the opportunists, of the routinization of the believers. If Tocqueville is to be believed, the functioning of the new democracy in America was conditional on the firm faith of these individualists. And yet, the firm institutionalization of Civil Society was based just as much on the routinization of that faith, its peaceful co-existence with a higher-level admission that truth was no one's monopoly. Social co-operation, loyalty and solidarity do not now presuppose a shared faith. They may, in fact, presuppose the absence of a wholly shared and seriously, unambiguously upheld conviction. They may require a shared doubt. Inner-directedness co-exists with a recognition of the legitimacy or even the obligation of an ultimate doubt. Inner authority is more effective than an external one, but it leads to an ultimate sovereignty of individual inquiry, and thereby also to scepticism. If the Cartesian consciousness is the ultimate court of appeal, it is free to reach the conclusion that the evidence available does not warrant a firm decision.

12

MODULAR MAN

There are firms which produce, advertise and market modular furniture. The point about such furniture is that it comes in bits which are agglutinative: you can buy one bit which will function on its own, but when your needs, income or space available augment, you can buy another bit. It will fit in with the one acquired previously, and the whole thing will still have a coherence, aesthetically and technically. You can combine and recombine the bits at will.

This makes modular furniture quite different from the ordinary kind: with the old kind, if you want coherence you have to buy it all at once, in one go, which means that you have to make a kind of irrevocable commitment, or at any rate a commitment which it will be rather costly to revoke. If you add a new bit of non-modular furniture to an old bit, you may end up with an eclectic, incoherent mess. Coherence is possible perhaps, but only attainable with difficulty, involving careful and possibly arduous search for new stylistically compatible items. You may then either resign yourself to messiness, or scrap the old and start altogether anew, which is costly.

The notion of Civil Society is being investigated in part by contrasting it with its available alternatives. The main point is that not one but more than one important contrast is involved. There is not only the opposition between liberal Civil Society and an ideological and exacting *Umma* (whether it be the dismally failed secular *Umma* of Marxism, or the strangely successful *Umma* of Islam), but also the contrast between Civil Society and the Fustelian society of ritual-based and communal, rather than doctrine-based and soteriological, society. What genuine Civil Society really requires is not modular furniture, but modular man.

The main point of Durkheimian sociology, and perhaps of the organicist or communalist tradition in social thought generally, is that in most contexts man is markedly un-modular. He belongs to a given culture and has internalized its values and assumptions: he is like a piece of furniture which is vividly marked by a given style. It is impossible to blend him effectively with men of a different cultural mould. He cannot be bonded into a social organism easily or at will. Some Social Contract theorists had supposed the opposite, and came close to imagining that a society could be set up as easily as modern man can buy a washing machine on hire purchase. A contract can easily be drawn up when it is to the advantage of both parties. On this culturally ethno-centric view, men are aim-pursuing individuals, who assess the environment surrounding them with a view to satisfying those aims: so they set up social institutions as instruments for furthering all this. Co-operation pays off, though there is a problem with ensuring delivery: logically, the best strategy is to receive co-operation but to refrain from fulfilling the contract. Such asymmetries must be prevented. There is a problem here: it is no use involving morality so as to explain and justify morality itself . . . So, the trouble with Social Contract theories was not merely that notoriously their position was logically circular – if only contracts propel men into socially responsible conduct, then a meta-contract is required to make the first one binding, and so on for ever – but above all, they were illegitimately generalizing from one *particular*, contract-prone kind of man, one who takes his own promises and commitments seriously, to man in general.

In a sense, the problem does not arise, at least in the beginning. Man in general is not modular, his individual isolated acts and affirmations are not to be taken very seriously or greatly to be relied on, his only real commitment is to a kind of interdependent and ritually orchestrated totality. Before you can trust his promise, it has to be made with trumpets and drama, with witnesses and presentations, dancing and music, and preferably with a sacrifice. His word is his bond only if blood flows while the word is given; and even then you had better be careful. Members of segmentary societies are treacherous. By laying on the solemnity, preferably with a sacrifice, by linking the act to all kinds of other social relationships, and symbolically fusing it with a whole network of solemn occasions, you can just about ensure that the commitment may be taken seriously – if you are lucky.

How is Civil Society possible at all? – to put the question in a Kantian form. The question can be spelt out more fully: how is it possible to have atomization, individualism, without a political emasculation of the atomized man (as in the world of Ibn Khaldun), and to have politically countervailing associations without these being stifling (as in the world of Fustel de Coulanges)? Miraculously, Civil Society does achieve both these aims. It is defined by such an achievement. Modularity of man is an illuminating way of referring to this condition.

Non-modularity obviates the possibility of choosing techniques simply in terms of clearly defined criteria of efficiency, and of nothing else. Instead it imposes the need to judge practices, if indeed they are to be subject to critical scrutiny at all, in terms of the multiple, imponderable, complex considerations of their participation in an indivisible, 'organic', cultural totality. It is this, of course, which leads romantics to admire undifferentiated many-sidedness and to spurn cost-benefit accountancy, with its specialized, distinct, isolated criteria of effectiveness. Man as desired by the romantics lives out the values of a culture; man as commanded by the utilitarians attends to the cost-benefit accountancy of life.

It is the political consequences of modularity which are really important. Modular man is capable of combining into effective associations and institutions, *without* these being total, many-stranded, underwritten by ritual and made stable through being linked to a whole inside set of relationships, all of these being tied in with each other and so immobilized. He can combine into specific-purpose, *ad hoc*, limited association, without binding himself by some blood ritual. He can leave an association when he comes to disagree with its policy, without being open to an accusation of treason. A market society operates not only with changing prices, but also with changing alignments and opinions: there is neither a just price nor a righteous categorization of men, everything can and should change, without in any way violating the moral order. The moral order has not committed itself either to a set of prescribed roles and relations, or to a set of practices. The same goes for knowledge: conviction can change, without any stigma of apostasy. Yet these highly specific, unsanctified, instrumental, revocable links or bonds are effective! The associations of modular man can be effective without being rigid!

It is *this* which makes Civil Society: the forging of links which are effective even though they are flexible, specific, instrumental. It does indeed depend on a move from Status to Contract: it means that men honour contracts even when they are not linked to ritualized status and group membership. Society is still a structure, it is not atomized, helpless and supine, and yet the structure is readily adjustable and responds to rational criteria of improvement. Modularity of man is the main answer to the question: how can there be countervailing institutions or associations which at the same time are not also stifling?

The origin of modular man constitutes an interesting problem. There are various theories concerning his genesis. Frequently, they invoke religion. A unique, jealous and monopolistic deity, especially one which had decided *a priori* the ultimate fates of the inhabitants of its creation, thereby preventing or rendering otiose any attempts at placation or propitiation, drives man into a solitude of terror in which all else pales into insignificance. If the individual living in terror of eternal damnation can provide evidence to himself indicating his own salvation, and if orderly conduct independent of external sanction and group pressure provides such evidence, the said individual (illogically treating something which is mere *evidence* concerning a fate already decided, as a *cause* which could help bring it about) will behave in a reliable, rule-bound manner, playing by the rules irrespective of other interests or pressures. In other words, he will become modular man. There are variants on this theory, such as those which stress the monastic ideal and its subsequent generalization and return into the world, under impact of protestant doctrine. Some theorists go further back and maintain that the individualism which underlies modernity was inherent in a symmetrical monotheism, in which the sacred deals with individual souls, not with collectivities.

We do not know which of these or other theories is correct, and it does not really matter for our present purposes: what matters for us is that modular man has emerged and helped bring about Civil Society. Perhaps one should add a refinement which will obviate a possible misunderstanding: in one sense, the member of segmentary society was also modular. He was transplantable and replaceable, as between one tribal segment and another, though only within the same culture. In fact, men banned in punishment for homicide or other serious transgression were welcomed and easily accepted into rival tribes and segments. Their very unacceptability in their milieu of origin, to which they could not return without risking death, made them loyal, reliable and hence attractive in their new unit.

But note: they were replaceable just because they were *similar* to all other individuals in the wider culture. Durk-

heim's notion of 'mechanical solidarity', based on the similarity of individuals and of sub-groups, underscores this
point. But modern modular man is not replaceable simply
because he is so stubbornly similar, because he will only be a
shepherd or peasant or whatever constitutes the normative
calling of his culture. On the contrary, he is highly variable,
not to say volatile, in his activities. He is modular because he
is capable of performing highly diverse tasks in the same
general cultural idiom, if necessary reading up manuals of
specific jobs in the general standard style of the culture in
question.

This is real modularity, quite different from the oafish
similarity of members of segmentary societies. Durkheim
can be reproached for implicitly lumping together the rigid
diversity of complex agrarian civilizations with the mobile
diversity of modern division of labour: so a modern market is
assimilated to a caste or *millet* society, both being called
'organic'. But one may also complain that Louis Dumont at
least gives the impression that mankind moves from a
traditional society which is both holistic and hierarchical to
modern individualism and egalitarianism. But segmentary
man, who does not receive adequate attention in such a
scheme, was holistic and egalitarian; his successor in complex but static civilizations was indeed both holistic and
hierarchical. It is only modern modular man who is both
individualistic and egalitarian, while nevertheless capable
both of effective cohesion against the state and of performing an amazing, indeed bewildering, diversity of tasks. It is
his emergence or reproduction which is the crucial problem
of Civil Society.

13

MODULAR MAN IS A NATIONALIST

The modularity of modern man was probably a pre-condition of the industrial miracle, and it is certainly – virtually by definition – a pre-condition of Civil Society. Civil Society is a cluster of institutions and associations strong enough to prevent tyranny, but which are, none the less, entered and left freely, rather than imposed by birth or sustained by awesome ritual. You can join (say) the Labour Party without slaughtering a sheep, in fact you would hardly be allowed to do such a thing, and you can leave it without incurring the death penalty for apostasy. When modern political parties were set up in newly independent Morocco in 1956, mountain tribes joined them in the old style, as they were habituated to doing with religious movements – they did so as collectivities, with an oath and a sacrifice. A clan not an individual would join a socialist party, and a bullock would perish in the process. This was a curious conflation of two distinct social idioms. The charismatic community which penalizes apostasy with death is a different matter again, and it cannot easily cohabit with Civil Society. The real *Umma* was and is altogether different in its moral intuitions, as the Western public learnt to its horror through the Rushdie affair.

But the modularity has a price, or at any rate a corollary, which in turn is liable to raise problems. So far, we have focused on certain moral and intellectual qualities which are presupposed by modularity: what is required is that a man should be capable of undertaking and honouring, and deeply internalizing commitments and obligations by a single and sober act. He will honour his debts and obligations without prolonged and fearful rituals, without involving the honour of all his kin, and so forth. It is not so much that his word is his bond, but that his word is his word even when spoken softly, without emphasis, in ordinary circumstances, without artificial heightening of the atmosphere. An employee of an insurance company once took pride in honouring a scribble he had lightly made over a dinner table – what he was showing was that all his expressions were binding.

He must also be capable of lucid, Cartesian thought, which separates issues rather than conflating them and takes them one at a time: the non-conflation of issues, the separating-out of the social strands, which makes society non-rigid, presupposes not merely a moral willingness, but also an intellectual capacity. It presupposes that capacity for segregating all separable issues and taking them one at a time, which Descartes stresses so much in his formulation of rules of intellectual comportment for modular man (though of course he did not use this expression). It does presuppose such abilities. Clear thought is not a birthright but an accomplishment, and somehow it had to be taught and its principles internalized: it is very much an acquired taste, and its acquisition had to be fostered. But there is also the price of isolation of one activity from another, a kind of fragmentation which leaves each activity unsustained by the others, cold and calculated by its own clearly formulated end, rather than part of a warm, integrated, 'total' culture. Such 'alienation' or 'disenchantment' is a price which some consider too high.

This is indeed one of the most important general traits of a modern society: cultural homogeneity, the capacity for context-free communication, the standardization of expression and comprehension. Citizens must be equal in culture as well as in basic status. This is presupposed both by mobility and hence the substitutability of men, and by the constant communication in an anonymous mass society between individuals unfamiliar with each other. The old segmentary societies of various kinds highlighted and fortified the boundaries between the segments by accentuated cultural differentiation: people spoke, ate, dressed, etc. differently according to their precise location in a complex, intricate social structure. They had to speak and generally comport themselves as their station or social location required, and to speak in any other manner would have been offensive presumption, if not a violation of legal or ritual prescription. In these conditions, there was not merely no incentive *for*, but plenty of reasons *against*, defining political units in terms of identity of culture. This idea, the new imperative of cultural homogeneity, which is the very essence of nationalism, goes against the grain of traditional society, and is generally absent from it. If ever it does exemplify a degree of correlation between political and cultural boundaries, it does so by accident, and not from any kind of inner compulsion.

Not so in the new realm of modular man. It cannot generally tolerate arbitrary semi-private or local semantic or syntactical conventions, which would restrict the possibility of transmission of messages only to some recipients in some circumstances. The conceptual currency must be standardized, not localized.

The standardization of idiom is in any case imposed on this kind of society by the nature of work within it, which ceases to be physical and becomes predominantly semantic: work is now the passing and reception of messages, largely between anonymous individuals in a mass society, who cannot normally be familiar with their interlocutors and their idiosyncrasies. Communication occurs, if not with man as such, then at any rate with man-as-standard-specimen-of-a-codified-culture. The equality of men before God is the ideological reflection of the equality of terminal points of a communication network. A Protestant religious style, an egalitarian and individual relation to the deity, is the theological echo of social modularity, just as the pervasive use of territorially and functionally localized mediators is the corollary of a segmented and rigid social order. The partner in the exchange of messages is located at the other end of a telephone or a fax, and his identity normally is not even known, let alone familiar. This being so, it is no longer technically feasible or acceptable that the partner's facial expression, body posture, past history and habits, location on a kinship map or a system of statuses should enter into the determination of the meaning of the message, as a kind of additional, localized but none the less essential phoneme. Private and idiosyncratic phonemes are *out*. This construction of meaning is obliged to draw exclusively from a non-contextual, shared, codified set of symbols.

In the old intimate, closed peasant communities, in which all speakers and listeners were deeply familiar with each other, these personal, privatized, localized phonemes were not merely tolerable, but were very nearly the only ones tolerated. Though language may in principle be, as Chomsky insists, the use of finite means for infinite ends, in actual practice much of mankind made use of finite, not to say extremely limited, means for finite ends. The infinite use of finite means was kept in reserve, remaining in the main an underexploited reserve in the human potential. That it should be so available, ready for use though seldom used, is something of a mystery; but it is a fact.

Modularity with its moral and intellectual pre-conditions makes Civil Society, the existence of non-suffocating, optional yet effective segments, possible; but it makes not only for a civil, but also for a nationalist society. In these circumstances, for the first time in world history a High Culture in this sense becomes the pervasive and operational culture of an entire society, rather than being at most the privilege and badge of a restricted social stratum. It is bound to define the limits of a society culturally and politically – for the enormous and costly educational machinery which makes all this possible also needs a political protector, paymaster and quality-controller. The state has not merely the monopoly of legitimate violence, but also of the accreditation of educational qualification. So the marriage of state and culture takes place, and we find ourselves in the Age of Nationalism.

All this also means, of course, that the territorial or social limits of the use of any one such High Culture at the same time define the limits of the substitutability, the possible deployment and social insertion, of any given modular individual who had received his training in that particular culture. For the average person, the limits of his culture are, if not quite the limits of the world, at any rate the limits of his employability, social acceptability, dignity, effective participation and citizenship. They define the limits of the use of his conceptual intuitions, access to the rules of the game, and to the intelligibility of the social world; beyond these limits, he becomes gaffe-prone, inept, subject to derision and contempt, and seriously handicapped in any endeavour. Hence his educationally acquired culture is by far his most important possession and investment, for it alone gives him access to all else; and the existence of a secure, preferably extensive political unit identified with that culture and committed to its protection and enforcement is his most pressing and powerful political concern. His deepest identity is determined neither by his bank balance nor by his kin nor by his status, but by his literate culture. He is not a nationalist out of atavism (quite the reverse), but rather from a perfectly sound though seldom lucid and conscious appreciation of his own true interests. He needs a politically protected *Gesellschaft*, though he talks of it in the idiom of a spontaneously engendered *Gemeinschaft*. The rhetoric of nationalism is inversely related to its social reality: it speaks of *Gemeinschaft*, and is rooted in a semantically and often phonetically standardized *Gesellschaft*.

At the beginning of the social transformation which brought about the new state of affairs, the world was full of political units of all sizes, often overlapping, and of cultural nuances, and hence of men whose own culture did not converge with the one used by the rulers of the sovereign political unit they inhabited – even assuming that sovereignty was neatly defined, which was seldom the case. Under the new social regime, this became increasingly uncomfortable. Men then had two options, if they were to diminish such discomfort: they could change their own culture, or they could change the nature of the political unit, either by changing its boundaries or by changing its cultural identification. Men generally adopted one or the other of these strategies, sometimes both, whether in succession or simultaneously. The surface result of all this was both the widespread centralizing cultural assimilation and the nationalist turbulence of the nineteenth and twentieth centuries.

14

FRIEND OR FOE?

The same or at any rate largely overlapping forces have produced both human modularity or individualism, and nationalism. (They are also responsible for the astonishing egalitarianism of modern society, which has inverted the long-standing or seemingly irreversible trend of complex societies towards ever-increasing social differentiation and accentuated, formalized hierarchy.) Modularity is the precondition of Civil Society and, according to the most famous and most influential sociological theory, it is itself in turn the fruit of Protestantism. The old religious order had in a way been much more comfortable, allowing the possibility of buying or serving one's way back into favour, but the severity of the new order encouraged men to become modular individualists. In all logic, predestination could and perhaps should also lead, as highlighted in James Hogg's *The Confessions of a Justified Sinner*, to an indulgent, totally permissive antinomianism.[1] If all is settled, why not sin to one's heart's content, if one is endowed with that crucial inner assurance of salvation? But, logically or not, most Protestants did not follow such a path. They took the path of conscientious restraint, self-policing, and thereby assisted or made possible the transition from coercive to productive society . . .

If Civil Society and nationalism are the offspring of the same forces, does this affinity turn them into political allies or enemies?

At the start, they did indeed tend to be allies. For one thing, early nationalism was inclined to be fairly modest and timid: such was the Herderian defence of the charms of folk cultures, against the arrogant and confident imperialism of

the French court or of British commercialism, or the bloodless universalism of the Enlightenment. The initial return to
totem pole, or rather village green, was defensive, almost
apologetic. Later, the philosophical anthropology of nationalism was to become more aggressive, not to say ferocious
and murderous, but that was yet to come.

But above all, initially liberalism and nationalism had the
same enemy, the baroque absolutist state, committed to the
hierarchy of ranks it both used and sustained, indifferent to
the folk cultures of its subjects, and in any case disinclined to
allow them too many liberties or too much participation. It
was given to centralization and bureaucratic order, but did
not wish or dare to touch the privileges of rank. So, the claim
for greater liberties for the individual, the ratification of the
civil rights of modular man, and the claim for greater
equality of cultures, could be and were presented jointly, and
were even seen as endowed with an elective affinity with
each other, as a joint pursuit of greater human fulfilment. In
1848, liberalism and nationalism could still be allies, even
brothers. The rights of individuals and the rights of cultures
could go hand in hand. Bureaucratic centralism threatened
local cultures, but it was no friend of individual liberty
either. The old *Landespatriotismus* of local estates could even
be an ally of the new ethnic nationalism, due in the end to
displace it. For instance, in Bohemia, a trans-ethnic *Bohemian*
patriotism could go hand in hand with *Czech* revendications
for cultural equality.

But in due course, the paths diverged. The individualism
inherent in the condition of modular man, if pushed to its
logical conclusion, was hostile to the cult of community.
This position was indeed pushed to its extreme logical
conclusion by those whose own social and political situation
impelled them in that direction. The finest formulations of
the liberal vision in the twentieth century came from Vienna,
where an individualist, intellectual and newly risen and newly

emancipated bourgeoisie clung, ironically, to a regime in which a softened erstwhile absolutism, once firmly linked to the Counter-Reformation, now became the only refuge of universalists who feared the new, closed, narrow nationalisms. It turned to this archaic polity from fear of the ethnically defined and collectivist new centrifugal forces. The medieval dynasty, which had turned itself into the champion of the Counter-Reformation, had taken this turn surprisingly early: already during the Napoleonic humiliation of the Germans, when the situation turned other Germans to nationalism, the Habsburgs, sensing the disaster nationalism spelt for their poly-ethnic dominions, kept aloof from the new trend.

Nationalism of the ethnic kind went in a different direction. It separated itself from *Landespatriotismus*, the effort to maintain the non-ethnic, territorial institutions of old local units. Notwithstanding the fact that its real social roots lay in the emergence of a mass anonymous society, destined to use a shared and standardized culture, it adopted the pretence (held in all sincerity by its protagonists and propagandists) that it was defending and perpetuating a village, folk culture. It had to do so: defending a newly created High Culture against the expansionism of the old one, it had to borrow the themes from local Folk Culture. It standardized and codified them and turned them into a High Culture, but did so in the name of the defence of the village against the old capital. In reality, it was creating a new, rich capital city and its culture. So, nationalism turned against liberalism even more than liberalism turned against nationalism.

In Central and Eastern Europe, nationalism was forced into this stance partly by the fact that new High Cultures had to be forged on the basis of peasant cultures. Neither ethnically defined polities nor local High Cultures ready to serve new national, i.e. culturally homogeneous, political units, were generally available. In other words, neither of the two partners in the intended marriage of state and culture was present: both had to be created. But the nationalists were hostile not merely to rival cultures, but also, and perhaps with special venom, to bloodless cosmopolitanism, probably in part because they perceived in it an ally of political centralism, and felt it to be a support for the old trans-national empires against neo-ethnic irredentism. They felt special loathing for those they considered to be the principal carriers of such cosmopolitanism. (They were right: in the end, the liberals committed to an open market in goods, in a sense men and ideas, were the last supporters of centralism, remaining faithful to it even when the old baroque absolutist partisans of the *ancien régime* had themselves given up the struggle.) But hostility to rootlessness went very deep in this movement, and cannot explained merely in terms of political opportunism.

So, in the later stages, the push towards an individualist Civil Society and the nationalist striving tended to come into collision with each other. The ambiguity of this relationship was most visible in the Habsburg empire, but the pattern was due in the end to be replayed in the Czarist-Bolshevik empire, especially so in the course of its final collapse. We do not yet know how this drama will end.

15

THE TIME ZONES OF EUROPE

The manner in which the nationalist aspect of modular humanity manifested itself in Europe varied from region to region. Roughly speaking, and allowing for certain complications, Europe falls into four time zones, resembling those global maps one sees at airports, which indicate the different times in the various vertically defined stretches of the globe.

It is perhaps useful, even if contrary to nature, to proceed from West to East, as in this matter the West is less problematical than the East. The Westernmost time zone is that of the Atlantic coast of Europe. The point about this zone is that from the late Middle Ages, if not earlier, it was occupied by strong dynastic states, which roughly, even if only very roughly, correlated with cultural areas. If nationalism requires the marriage of state and culture, then in this zone the couple had been cohabiting long before their union was acclaimed by nationalist Manifest Destiny. This meant that when, with the coming of nationalism, political units had to adjust themselves to cultural boundaries, no very great changes other than a kind of *ex post* ratification were required. History had made a present to nationalism of a broad region where the nationalist imperative was already, at least in considerable measure, satisfied before the event. Some turbulence there was, of course, even within this zone: to this day, there is violence in Bilbao and Belfast.

One major adjustment of the political map has indeed taken place, namely the establishment of the Republic of Ireland. But all in all, the map of this part of Europe in the age of nationalism does not look so very different from what it had been in the age when dynasty, religion and local community had been the determinants of boundaries. The dynastic states, finding themselves in charge of an area correlating with a culture, tended to identify with that culture in some measure even before nationalism had turned culture into the most potent political symbol. There was no need for very widespread ethnic irredentism when the new order arrived. New cultures did not need to be created, and the attempt to revive one in Ireland failed. The cultures which exist did not need to acquire new political roofs: the roof was ready, waiting for them. Nationalism did not draw on peasant cultures so as to invent a new literate one: rather, it strove to replace peasant idioms by an existing court or urban speech. 'Peasant' in this area is still more a term of abuse than the name of the idealized carrier of ethnic identity and national culture. Peasants had to be turned into proper-speaking nationals, but no national High Cultures needed to be forged from peasant materials. Wordsworth may prefer country folk and their speech to Augustan formality, but the nation of Shakespeare did not need to be endowed with a newly codified culture. Had Wordsworth been, say, Czech, it would have been a different story altogether. But these Westernmost nations needed no Awakeners. Induced forgetfulness rather than invented memory was the national bond, as Ernest Renan insisted.[1]

The next zone to the East was different. Far from possessing ready-made dynastic states, it was an area of quite exceptional political fragmentation, endowed with effective political units much smaller than the geographical extension of the two locally dominant High Cultures. The major political meta-unit of the area, the Holy Roman Empire, had long ago lost any effective reality, and by the time of the coming of the age of nationalism had ceased to exist even in name. But if the region lacked pre-existing political units ready for the nationalist requirements, it was exceedingly well equipped with pre-existing, codified, normative High

Cultures. Both Italian and German were well codified, ever since the Renaissance and the Reformation respectively, at the latest. The cultural bride was all ready and tarted up at the altar, only the political groom had to be found and his claims made good.

So here there was indeed a need for polity-building, though not for culture-building. There was no real need for schoolteachers, ethnographers, folklorists and national Awakeners generally to go out to the villages and construct a national culture from the chaos of regional dialectal variety, though the folklorists were busy at work. But the cultural ethnogenesis had all largely taken place before political nationalism appeared on the scene. Whereas in the Westernmost zone all that needed to be done was to transform peasants, sunk in local cultural particularism, into properly educated members of the national culture, here (though this also had to be done to some extent) the main thing needed was a political change. An existing High Culture had to be endowed with a political roof worthy of it and capable of giving it shelter. It took a certain amount of military and diplomatic activity, but not much else. By the later part of the nineteenth century, the task had been accomplished.

It was the next time zone to the East which presented the greatest problems from the viewpoint of the implementation of the nationalist principle of *one culture, one state*. Here there was an appallingly complex patchwork of diverse cultures, intermixed both geographically and in the social structure, with political, cultural and religious boundaries devoid of any coherence or mutual support. Many of the peasant cultures were not clearly endowed with a normative High Culture at all. Some even had no name. They often lacked educational institutions capable of engendering, protecting, perpetuating and disseminating it, in a world in which High Cultures had to become co-extensive with entire socities, instead of defining a restricted minority. Here both cultures and polities had to be created, an arduous task indeed. Nationalism began with ethnography, half descriptive, half normative, a kind of salvage operation and cultural engineering combined.[2] If the eventual units were to be compact and reasonably homogeneous, more had to be done: many, many people had to be either assimilated, or expelled or killed. All these methods were eventually employed in the course of implementing the nationalist political principle, and they continue to be in use.

Finally, there is Europe's fourth time zone, corresponding more or less to the territories of the erstwhile Czarist empire. The pattern here follows fairly closely that of the third zone – but only until the end of the First World War. Thereafter the two paths diverge. The Czarist empire, unlike the others which disappeared for ever, was soon re-established under entirely new management and in the name of a uniquely new, formally secular ideology, though one endowed with all the zeal and messianism of a salvation religion. The new faith was imposed with conviction and utter ruthlessness, and generated a secular *Umma*, a charismatic community which saw its task on earth as the implementation of absolute righteousness, and which believed itself possessed of the unique and infallible recipe for the attainment of such righteousness.

The faith which was being implemented had undergone, under the leadership and inspiration of Lenin, a kind of inverse Reformation: initially, the faith possessed no clauses which would entail an internal stratification of the faithful. The original Marxist doctrine contained no recommendation for the creation of a privileged priesthood. All men eventually – and in the meantime at any rate all the oppressed and dispossessed – were granted an equal and symmetrical access and relationship to the truth which was to save humanity.

Lenin, however, had come to the conclusion that ordinary

humanity was incapable of rising to the perception of the truth (i.e. the unaided working class would merely be reformist rather than revolutionary, and would concentrate on improving its position within the existing social order, rather than grasp that its role was to usher in a wholly new condition). This being so, a specially dedicated and highly disciplined religious order was required, capable of understanding, appreciating and implementing the great message. Lenin blended the messianic Marxist vision of the role of the proletariat with a more distinctively Russian vision of a dedicated revolutionary *corps d'élite*. Such a body was indeed forged by this Ignatius Loyola of Marxism.

When, rather surprisingly, the revolution succeeded and, even more surprisingly, survived despite the absence of external aid from fraternal revolutions elsewhere, this order naturally inherited the governance of all the Russians, and proceeded to perform the task which had thus fallen to it in a manner befitting the possessor of an absolute and supremely important Revelation. As Lenin observed, the teaching of Marx was all-powerful because it was true. A red banner with this quotation continued to hang prominently in the entrance hall of the Institute of Philosophy of the Academy of Sciences of the USSR well into the late perestroika period, by which time however it was impossible to draw it to the attention of any passing Soviet citizen or scholar without provoking a wry smile.

Under this dedicated and determined leadership, the new secular *Umma* had even less difficulty in containing nationalist irredentism than had the empires of the erstwhile Holy Alliance during the century which stretched from 1815 to 1918. The new ideocracy and the institutions it spawned controlled the entire territory with ease, and obliged its inhabitants to proclaim that their nationalist aspirations were satisfied. This fiction was maintained well into the 1980s, and deceived even otherwise intelligent commentators.[3]

A complication of some importance which must also be recorded is that as a result of its military victory in 1945 the Socialist *Umma* pushed the boundary of the fourth zone westwards, and incorporated large areas which had belonged to the third zone between 1918 and the Second World War. Moscow time, ideologically and politically speaking, now extended to the Adriatic and the Elbe.

For reasons which are of the greatest importance, but which have not been adequately elucidated and which are discussed elsewhere in this volume, the world's first secular ideocracy collapsed in the late 1980s, making plain that the faith in this particular salvation creed had disappeared almost completely in the lands in which its implementation had been attempted so seriously. Many now crave a return to stability and security and international prestige: *no one* laments the lost faith. The Homeland of the Revolution became the location of its most emphatic and ignominious burial. It is of course this collapse which set free that craving for Civil Society, which is our principal theme. Equally, it released nationalism.

16

THE VARIETIES OF NATIONALIST EXPERIENCE

There is a sense in which the third time zone provides the clearest illustration of the normal human condition when it is not distorted by special circumstances: the transition from the condition in which culture does underwrite status but not political boundaries, to the new condition in which it does the very reverse – when it ignores or suspends status, but underlines and sharpens political boundaries. This metamorphosis or transition from tradition to nationalism is most conspicuously manifest in this zone, where it is least obscured by contingent intrusions – either by the accidental presence of dynastic states which just happen to correspond roughly to future national ones, or by the fortuitous presence of a well-codified High Culture, or by the Second Coming of Ideocracy in a secular guise. It is the third zone which proceeded directly from a blatantly ethnicity-defying, dynastic-religious order to a rabid nationalism. In this sense, the stages through which it passed can be considered 'normal' – they exemplify what one would expect if no unusual additional factors are operative.

There is the first stage in which the old dynastic-religious system is still in place, as it was at the Congress of Vienna in 1815. The bureaucratic centralization and standardization imposed by the Enlightened despots of the eighteenth century, without any nationalist motivation, nevertheless already engendered that link between government and culture which impels men towards nationalism. The old order remains in place, but the snake has entered the Garden of Eden, even though it is as yet a timid and relatively inconspicuous snake. That was not to last.

There is the second stage of sustained but all in all not too effective nationalist irredentism, when the new principle of the exclusive legitimacy of culture-based states makes itself felt, though it cannot yet prevail against the established order, except in places where the established order is particularly weak. This was the state of affairs between the 1820s and 1918. Except for the Balkans, where the unusual weakness of the Ottoman empire eventually permitted the creation of five or six more or less national buffer states, nationalism was not unduly successful in politics. But it was enormously successful in culture: it conquered men's hearts and its legitimacy was widely accepted.

Stage three is interesting: it could be called the age of nationalism triumphant and self-defeating. It lasted from 1918 till the domination of Europe by Hitler and Stalin in the course of the Second World War. It was characterized by a political system consisting of fairly small states, overtly and proudly self-defined as national, which had succeeded the old poly-ethnic, religiously validated empires. These new states had all the weaknesses of the old empires – they were just as haunted by minorities as the old empires had been, if not more so. In addition, they were cursed with a whole series of additional weaknesses of their own. They were small; they were in the main new, and were not hallowed by age; they were often led by inexperienced, greedy and incautious ruling classes, eager to make hay while the sun shone, without expectation of or much concern with stability, or with insurance against changes of wind; and they had among their minorities members of the erstwhile dominant ethno-linguistic groups, unhabituated to submission and minority status, resentful of it, and endowed with external support in their 'home' national state, which helped and encouraged them to struggle against their newly attributed subordinate status. The consequences of these manifold weaknesses soon became only too visible: the system offered virtually no effective resistance (except for the case of Finland), when the two great dictators of the century agreed to carve it up between themselves. The system of supposedly national states, set up in the name of national self-determination in 1918 and 1919, collapsed like a house of cards.

The time when it collapsed was also the period of an unprecedentedly large-scale and total war, in the course of which both the flow of information and the authority of moral susceptibilities were markedly diminished. This was stage four. A century of ineffective national striving, followed by a quarter of a century during which the roles of oppressor and oppressed were in part inverted, left the region a seething mass of ethnic resentments.

On top of all that, the dominant power, Hitler's Germany, was committed to a mixture of a communalist and a biological ideology, which singled out certain ethnic minorities without a territorial or peasant base, and hence devoid of the virtue-conferring *Voelk*ish qualities, as specially noxious and deserving extermination. The interstitial position with which the most important of such minorities was endowed had in any case made it an object of hatred among the 'host' populations.

The hatred and resentments were there, as was the ideological rationale, and as it happens so was the political will, the opportunity and the organizational machinery. Wartime secrecy made it all easier. The consequence is known. The Jews, but not only they, were the object of a massive, well-organized and efficient campaign of extermination. Other populations suffered as well, and during the immediate post-war period, though information now flowed more easily, nevertheless indignation and the desire for retaliation permitted the employment of methods – above all, forcible transplantation of populations and disregard of normal principles of justice, accompanied by some murder – as a result of which in some though not all regions the previously complex ethnic map was brought into closer relationship with the newly imposed political boundaries. It came to satisfy at least in some places the requirements of nationalism, the imperative of cultural homogeneity within any one political unit, far more closely than had been feasible in days of moral restraint. This was stage four. It could be called, to use a term which came into use in the course of the Yugoslav civil wars of the early 1990s, the time of ethnic cleansing.

So much for stage four. Thanks to the crimes of Hitler and Stalin, some though not all areas of Eastern Europe now satisfied the nationalist imperative. At the same time, when included in the extended area of domination of the new secular ideocracy, it did not matter too much whether or not they did satisfy that imperative, because the new empire had the will and the means to impose its authority in any case, both in areas in which murder and transplantation had produced ethnic homogeneity, and in areas in which the old complexity continued to prevail. Hitler's policies of murder contributed to the tidying up of the ethnic map. The forcible transplantation of populations which took place under Stalin's direct or indirect rule sometimes did so (notably in Poland and Czechoslovakia), but inside the Soviet Union proper it only changed the patterns of ethnic complexity, rather than diminishing it.

Stage five is something which may partake of both wishfulfilment and reality: there are signs of it having taken place in at least large parts of Western Europe (though not everywhere), and even in some areas to the east of it. In advanced industrialism, the intensity of ethnic feeling diminishes. At any rate it diminishes between populations not too distant from each other in the extent to which they benefit from the advantages of industrial affluence. There is at least an element of truth in the Convergence Thesis, which claimed that industrial cultures eventually come to resemble each other. This may not be true if the initial base line is very different – Atlantic and East Asian prosperity may or may not have similar cultural accompaniments – but it does seem to be true if the starting point has the degree of affinity which can be credited to European nations. Moreover, in advanced industrialism, inter-communal jealousy is no longer fed so powerfully by economic jealousy: the distance between the very affluent and the very, very affluent is not so provocative as the distance which once obtained between the indigence of early entrants to industrialism and its first beneficiaries. (The acute form of difference is still liable to hold true of the relationship between migrant workers and host populations, and the hope of diminished hostility does not, alas, apply there.)

A certain cultural affinity – cultures now differing only phonetically rather than semantically, using different words for similar notions – plus diminished economic resentment, may lead to a lessening of the political salience of ethnicity. Something of this has happened in parts of Western and even Central Europe, in areas where a war concerning national frontiers is now far less conceivable than it had been early in the century. Only too obviously this is not the case in, say, erstwhile Yugoslavia, but one may only hope that the same curve of development will some time also come to apply. Whether it can only do so *after* ethnic cleansing is a sad question.

The point about what we have called the fourth time zone of Europe – the area where neither the political bridegroom nor the cultural bride was available for the required marriage of nation state and national culture, but where the search for them was delayed by seventy or forty years of Bolshevik ideocracy – is that it shared with zone three the first two stages, but that it then came to be politically frozen. Prince Mikhail Sergeevich Gorbachev chose to awaken the Sleeping Beauty, only to be rudely shaken by her un-gentle, un-princess-like reaction when aroused. His hesitancy in committing himself fully to so pushy a partner provided his rival Prince Boris with his chance, which he seized without hesitation, and it certainly enabled him to dispose of the more hesitant suitor. Yeltsin ruthlessly allied himself to the nationalists of the non-Russian republics to deprive Gorbachev of his base in the Union government, and inherited residual Russia. But it is far from obvious yet whether even he can mollify the dangerous lady sufficiently to be spared himself.

17

EASTERNMOST ZONE RESUMED

During the second half of the 1980s, the new secular soteri-ological ideocracy collapsed, in some measure because of internal opposition, but in the main because of a loss of conviction and nerve at its centre. The leaders, faced with sustained defeat in both the consumerist and the arms races, turned to liberalization in the hope of a quick – or the only – remedy, and found themselves incapable of arresting its course once it had gathered momentum, or at any rate were laudably unwilling to adopt the extreme measures which would have been required to arrest it. In the days of faith, their predecessors would not have hesitated to use them, but ruthlessness on such a scale no longer seems to come so easily (to their great credit) to members of this political culture. Their enemies liked to characterize them as a sect of men good at nothing other than the maintenance of a monopoly of power, and wholly dedicated to that end. Once it was indeed so, but time and experience had some-how endowed them with a new and fateful moral fastidious-ness. I had always feared and anticipated that when finally defeated and humbled in the international, mainly economic race, they would fall back on insulation and blackmail: if you do not pay us Danegeld, we shall commit collective suicide and take you with us, or at any rate pursue a policy which only leaves you the option of either suicide or at least partial submission. They did not choose this course (at least as yet), one which would not have repelled their political predecessors, and we must be deeply grateful for this newly acquired moral restraint on their part and hope it has become habit-forming.

The authoritarian system collapsed, not totally but sufficiently to reveal both the yearning for Civil Society and the powerful ethnic passions. It is the interaction and the relative strength of these two newly liberated forces which concerns us. At present, their interaction makes up much of the great political drama of Eastern Europe, and the outcome is far from clear. But it is already possible to make a certain number of observations.

Both the economic and the political aspects of Civil Society are rather difficult to bring into being. Initial political parties tend to be ephemeral clubs of intellectuals, without effective grass roots. It is easy enough to stimulate certain types of enterprise, notably the kind of service industry which tends already to exist in semi-legal form in all but the most repressive and total of dictatorships. A small restaurant requires little space, not a great deal of entrepreneurial talent or imagination – not much more than a certain amount of gastronomic and visual taste and fastidiousness. But a genuine open market, as opposed to mere networks, needs an entrepreneurial class and institutions – and it does not seem easy to set these up by fiat. And much the same goes for political institutions.

On the other hand, ethnically based and defined associations appear to be capable of almost immediate formation and firm as well as rapid crystallization. Solid organization with local branches, shared symbols and sentiments, recognized and respected leadership – it seems to be possible to create these on a nationalist foundation with amazing speed and effectiveness. This may be regrettable: one might wish that the other aspects of modular man, other than his passionate eagerness to identify with his distinctive cultural category, and to ensure that his institutional milieu is convergent with his own culture, should make as ready an appearance. The fact is they do not. We may like this or not, but we have to recognize it. The sleeping beauty of ethnicity can, alas, often be awakened with the gentlest and most tender of kisses. She now sleeps ever so lightly. The sleeping beauty of Civil Society may be much more deeply and genuinely desirable, at least to those sharing our taste, but to wake her effectively is the devil's own job.

Once again, are nationalism and liberalism allies? At first, certainly: faced with an authority which combines dogmatism with centralism, those who long for free thought and those who long for autonomy for their own cultural totem pole will naturally form an alliance against the centre. But later . . .?

Given the speed with which ethnicity can be mobilized, and the slowness with which anything else can be set up, it is probably a good thing to use ethnic bases as fortresses against centralist reaction. This was in effect Boris Yeltsin's strategy in his confrontation with Gorbachev. Some of us doubted the wisdom of such indiscriminate encouragement of ethnic particularism, which involved a weakening of the centre at any cost; but when, in August 1991, both Yeltsin and Gorbachev had to be saved against a would-be violent reaction by the centrists, it was Yeltsin's ability to fall back on such a base which saved the day. Similarly, by the end of the year, he could use the same force to destroy the institutional base of Gorbachev's position and triumph over him. The price nationalism will exact for all this still remains to be seen.

One can sum it all up as follows: the modularity of man, so intimately tied up with an industrial and growth-oriented society, has two aspects, two principal social corollaries: it makes *possible* Civil Society, the existence of countervailing and plural political associations and economic institutions, which at the same time are not stifling; and it also makes *mandatory* the strength of ethnic identity, arising from the fact that man is no longer tied to a specific social niche, but is instead deeply linked to a culturally defined pool. The one potentiality is a mere option, essential presumably in the long term if the society is to be capable of competing with its rivals, but not always overwhelmingly strong in the short run; the other, however, constitutes an immediately and powerfully felt imperative. This is a fact, whether or not we like it.

18

A NOTE ON ATOMIZATION

Atomization of human society has been a persistent fear and sometimes a hope, and occasionally both at once. One tradition saw man as alone at first, with society only artificially bringing men into co-operative association. A more realistic account begins with a kind of natural togetherness, with a more sophisticated social order modifying it, and allowing the individual more leeway. Some of the theorists of atomization are of relevance to our argument.

Plato has been accused by his most interesting critic, Popper, of being imbued with nostalgia for the Closed Society, by which Popper clearly means communal, tribal society. Though what *The Republic* envisages is in scale and spirit akin up to a point to tribal society, in fact the methods Plato commends to ensure its stability and perpetuation are rather those of an *Umma*: there is absolute and transcendent doctrine, and the leadership is ascribed to what looks very much like a doctrinal rather than a traditional, ritual-oriented clerisy. Virtue is made the object of the state, on a Spartan model: and the virtue is of the ascetic, abnegation kind. At best, it is all a curious mixture of a pre-Axial community and a doctrinal, absolutist, soteriological *Umma*.

What is interesting for our purposes is that Plato anticipates its atomization and disintegration at very nearly the end of the process of decline, as its near-terminal end prior to the final abomination of tyranny. It is a consequence and accompaniment of ideological pluralism and liberalism, of 'democracy' in which *anything* goes and intellectually everything is permitted and practised. The barrier against it is Reason, envisaged as a compulsive inner agency, socially and psychically as well as logically. Faith, hierarchy and discipline are its additional supports. Plato's Reason is not at all like that of the modern empiricists, for whom theories are underdetermined by facts, which in the end renders Reason modest, tentative and sceptical in its affirmations. His Reason is emphatic and final, engendering unique, determinate and compelling conclusions, sharing these traits with religious Revelation, capable of producing a rich harvest of fully authenticated truths, strong enough to provide firm guidance for social life.

Ibn Khaldun, in the fourteenth century, comes closer to the social context with which we are concerned. There is a marked similarity to Plato, though he is endowed with rather more sociological realism. Atomization for him is not so much pathological as the natural, inevitable and constant consequence of civilization, of urban living, a sophisticated economy and the division of labour. Tyranny as a consequence of urban atomization is the natural condition of city life. But it leads to submission to government external to the city itself, rather than to chaos. Plato was in effect concerned with and inspired by a semi-commercial city state, in which the institutions and absence of centralization of tribal society co-exist with the corrosive effects of trade. Ibn Khaldun was inspired by quite a different world, in which a fully commercialized city, concerned with the economy, co-existed with 'uncorrupted' tribalism which more or less monopolized the polity.

Ibn Khaldun is entirely at one with Plato as seeing urbanization as the consequence of the desire for more than a minimal subsistence standard of living, but there is a difference: Plato goes on to offer a recipe for saving those seduced by urbanization from moral degeneration, and holds this to be feasible, even though difficult. Ibn Khaldun indulges in no such illusions, and believes that there is no way at all of avoiding the price of urbanization, which is lack of cohesion and community, and a kind of total political emasculation.

He makes no attempt to offer any recipes for warding off such a fate, and there is nothing to suggest that it entered his head that such a thing could ever be found. He is much more of a positive sociologist than a normative philosopher, and contents himself with describing what actually does happen in the world as he knows it. The atomized town-dwellers are incapable of maintaining, running or defending a polity, but they are supplied with rulers capable of all these things, from that reservoir of political and military talent, namely the tribal countryside. Personnel rotate, but the structure does not change.

What is interesting is that Ibn Khaldun saw urban and market society as inherently anomic, in Durkheim's term, and atomized. He saw this society as being exploited by government, rather than using government as its agent. The possibility of a Civil Society, of associations within the city strong enough to resist the state (or even to turn it into its servant) does not seem to have occurred to him. It really does transcend the limits of his political imagination, or indeed the realistic options of the society he knew. Modular man, capable of loyalty, cohesion, and hence political effectiveness, without for all that being locked into an over-cohesive tribal community composed of real or putative kin, is a possibility he simply does not contemplate. Notwithstanding the 'protestant' traits of Islam, this development does not seem to have occurred in the Muslim world and to this day is not very much in evidence.

We proceed straight to Marx, who is obviously relevant here, though he is a complex example, and perhaps less than coherent on this important topic. Marx's values and background philosophical anthropology seem to be a strange blend of communalism and anarchism: for him atomization is not unambiguously a bad thing. It is of course credited to the market, and to that extent Marx would fit into the tradition of Plato and Ibn Khaldun, which sees the market as antithetical to genuine society. For Ibn Khaldun, however, it was the ungoverned wilderness which produced political man in the form of tribesman: for Marx, the order-less social anarchy of the industrial melting-pot gives birth to true humanity, and the one class destined to liberate mankind from self-imposed chains. But at the same time, it seems that it is the atomization of the proletariat which turns it into the tool which will liberate mankind from pathological social forms, which both deprives and frees it from particularist loyalties. Thus it becomes a paradigm of the human species-being, the universal and liberating class. Spurious Civil Society had deprived its labour of both inherent meaning and any links to a moral community, by treating it as a mere commodity. The market is formally just and free, but is slanted in favour of some: the state, likewise, purports to be a guardian of fair play, but is covertly at the service of the victorious beneficiaries of the formally equal but substantially biased procedures of Civil Society. This Calvary is said to purify proletarian man and make him able to restore a world in which work will once again have a meaning, and will not be linked to constraint, nor require its protection.

In the new order to be established in the future by the proletariat, automatic harmony (a curious echo and extrapolation or exaggeration of the harmony credited by the liberals to the market?) is combined with utter individualism, with men freed from constraints of ascribed and imposed social roles, and able to do whatever they fancy at freely chosen times. Atomization and total freedom remain, but are mysteriously combined with social harmony and productivity, and no longer engender any need for authority as a barrier to chaos and violence. The only concrete image on which this ideal can be based is the artistic Bohemia, the traditional counter-culture of the bourgeoisie, with its ritualized contempt for bourgeois punctuality and for its deference to the obligations inherent in each role. Behind Marx, one senses the presence of Heine. The only concrete information Marx offers us of the social life of liberated humanity is an extrapolation of Bohemian defiance of role-obligation, sartorially, sexually and in other ways. No timetable is to inhibit and thwart free, spontaneous, polymorphous activity. But it is interesting to note that, in Marx, atomization plays a role both in specifying the mechanics of social development and in helping to define that ideal condition which, as its presupposed contrast, makes sense of the rejection of the actual order. The proletariat is atomized here and now, which helps create the revolutionary situation; but men will also be perfect yet non-antagonistic individualists in the classless society. Atomization seems to have both a positive and a negative aspect.

There is of course also Durkheim's use of the term *anomie* to offer his version of the notion of social atomization. He appeared to think of it as a condition allowing of degrees, and liable to haunt modern society to a greater or smaller extent.

The interest of the notion in the present context is this: the crisis which has led to the re-emergence of the idea of Civil Society as a standard and as an ideal is one in which the fear of atomization was for once exceedingly realistic. The previous fears have generally been all at once exaggerated, and presupposed a rather utopian contrast. The disintegration of the ritual unity of the ancient city did not lead, as Plato feared, to a 'democratic' free for all: rather, it eventually led, for better or for worse, to a world religion. The political supineness of the Muslim city did indeed mean that autonomous cities or bourgeois regimes failed to emerge in the Muslim world, though the internal structurelessness of the city was perhaps not quite as total as a simple-minded reading of Ibn Khaldun would suggest. The Ottoman version of Muslim society did not allow the productive element to take part in government, but it did allow and even oblige it to organize itself in internally self-administering *millet* (or a set of them), so that it did not altogether lack structure. Neither the proletariat nor the bourgeoisie of capitalist industrialism has manifested in the long run that total melting-pot quality with which Marx credited either or both of them. But there is one place where something like near-total atomization did occur, and that was in the 'real socialism' of the Communist world, as it existed prior to its dissolution by perestroika. It was this above all which breathed new life into the notion of Civil Society: it re-emerged, to speak Marxese, as the negation of the negation of Civil Society.

The point seems to be that in the modern world such atomization is for once more feasible than it had ever been in the past, and at the same time less necessary and less functional. It is feasible because the traditional state, however tyrannical or absolutist in its pretensions, simply did not possess the technical equipment for pervading the whole of social life. Whatever might just about be possible within its military barracks or slave-manned plantations, in the main effective control required the use of local institutions as mediators, and they inevitably acquired some measure of autonomy. The transport, communication and surveillance technology then available did not make real totalitarianism feasible in the old traditional world. The irony of 'real socialism' was that the socialist fusion of productive, political and ideological hierarchies with the ideocratic monopoly of association, aided by modern administration and communication networks, really led, not to a newly restored social man, but to something closer to total atomization than perhaps any previous society had known. Social control worked by deliberately implicating virtually everyone in moral and economic dirt: everyone was required to express support for the persecution of dissidents, in the mouthing of sacred truths, and the economic system encouraged everyone to take part in illicit practices. With everyone guilty and contaminated both morally and legally, the likelihood of dissent inspired by moral indignation was diminished. The state made sure that there were few candidates for casting the first stone. Only a furtive, opportunist, demoralizing tendency towards networks of mutual assistance remained outside the *pays légal*: a feeble and unsavoury *pays réel*, incapable of inspiring much affection or deep loyalty. It was this, alongside the loathing of the totalitarian *pays légal*, which endowed the idea of Civil Society with its potent resonance and strong appeal.

Near-total atomization has thus now become technically feasible. It is the sad achievement of the Soviet Union and its satellites to have demonstrated this. A society which wills itself to be an *Umma* – i.e. to be the implementation of a unique and rectitude-defining Revelation, a charismatic community which seeks to ensure righteousness on earth and suppresses corruption, and which makes virtue the aim of the state – can and does atomize itself in the pursuit of this aim.

The uniqueness of the revelation and its absolutization led to a near-total absence of political pluralism, and the fact that economic pluralism was excluded by the actual content of the doctrine also made its crucial contribution to this outcome. The result was a winner-takes-all world, largely devoid of independently attainable economic prizes and, with all the political prizes concentrated in a single game, a ruthless struggle for the control of one unique hierarchy. This on its own would in any case lead to complete unscrupulousness in the political game: it would be utter folly in such a system to allow losers to survive and attempt to reverse the verdict of the previous battle. The black-and-white, total quality of politics was a natural outcome: the mystery is that during its final period the system softened considerably, and eliminated politicians in the end faced retirement

rather than the firing squad. But significantly, this routinization also led – unlike random terror – to virtually complete
erosion of faith. The old religions seem to survive routinization and even thrive on it: the secular revelation of Marxism
seems to be unable to do this.

The totality of the claims of the faith, plus the content of
the faith, which excluded economic pluralism, had similar
consequences. The *Umma*-status of the entire order required
this game to be played with enormous pretensions to absolute morality: the victor could not be characterized as simply
the least bad alternative in difficult and ambiguous circumstances, or as the beneficiary of chance, who had better be
tolerated and given support out of respect for the continuity
of the system – as the outcome of an unfortunate election is
liable to be tolerated in Civil Society, even if everyone
knows that, owing to some vagary of the electoral system,
the result is undesirable and perhaps extremely bad. By a
well-known style of circular reasoning, the invocation of the
oft-affirmed superiority of substantive or class justice over
more formalistic procedural propriety, the outcome was for
the time being presented as the voice of absolute reason on
earth. The losers had to be sinners and heretics and Enemies
of the People. Of course, the outcome can be, and often is,
disavowed subsequently, when 'distortions' of the system
are corrected. The same or similar abuse is then redistributed.
This led among other things to the somewhat comic and
undignified habit of regularly renaming cities, squares, thor-
oughfares, bridges and railway stations. You might say that a
real Civil Society is one which does not rechristen all its
railway stations and boulevards and issue a new city plan
each time the government changes. It names its thorough-
fares after fallible people and does not need to rechristen the
locations when the bearers of the names are deprived of
infallibility.

19

THE END OF A MORAL ORDER

In an important sociological and non-evaluative sense, the Bolshevik system did constitute a moral order. By contrast, and this is perhaps one of its most significant virtues, Civil Society is an a-moral order.

Under the Communist system, truth, power and society were intimately fused. Political authority was not seen as a convenience, but as the fulfilment and agent of an ultimate, immeasurably deep insight into the nature of the human condition and of the historic plan, and the agent of its implementation. It was the caretaker of absolute righteousness, deputizing for it and preparing the ground for its coming. Its aim was total virtue, not the diminution of inconvenience. In logical consequence, opposition to it was naturally not merely some kind of civil offence, like driving on the wrong side of the road; it was a vicious and deep disturbance of the moral order. It deserved and received a far more emphatic condemnation. 'For dogs, a dog's death!' – the headlines screamed at the time of the Moscow trials.

How could such a position be maintained? It is not really all that difficult. First of all what you need is some central intuition which has an inherent plausibility, a moral as well as an intellectual appeal. The idea that history exemplifies a plan, that at the end of it mankind will be free from both oppression and exploitation, that the individual or sectional control and use of nature for private ends is wrong, and that we should all co-operate for a common end, that such is the right and proper and natural ordering of society, while competition and use of resources for private ends is socially pathological – all this is not without its appeal or even some plausibility. Ever since Condorcet and Hegel, the idea of history as providence has been one of the most popular of God-surrogates.

It is not unreasonable either to anticipate that the attainment of so noble an end should also be difficult, and that it should provoke enmity, notably from those whose own interests lead them to oppose progress. The existence of such enemies is not accidental, but part of the essential plot of history. God entails Satan. History would not be a meaningful drama if there were no deep conflict at the heart of it. But the fact that the enemies are in one sense necessary to the scheme of things does not mean that they are not genuinely and profoundly evil. Such enemies will stop at nothing, at no means however foul, and the struggle with them can hardly be less than ruthless. The enemies will shamelessly invoke spurious ideals such as formal liberty, procedural propriety, human rights. But when there is but one basic battle, between the partisans of the ultimate human liberation and their opponents, then to be distracted or to allow oneself to be weakened by a concern with the methods used, by the ultimately dishonest appeal to spurious formal and procedural principles – that would be the last and greatest treason! It would be the sign of most culpable and unforgivable weakness to allow oneself to be diverted by such spurious morality.

Facts are generally ambiguous. In normal circumstances, an individual cannot but take most of his convictions from his social environment. No man can carry out the Cartesian programme of re-creating his world without indebtedness to unchecked social prejudice. He might perhaps individually check this fact or that; he cannot verify the lot. Theories are underdetermined by facts, as philosophers like to tell us; what they generally fail to add is that coercion and social pressure take up the slack. Nothing else can possibly do it. The leeway allowed by the lack of logical compulsion is made up by social compulsion. (If Durkheim were to be believed, logical compulsion is but a hidden form of social compulsion anyway.) If it were not, if culture did not prejudge questions which in the nature of the case remain open, the individual would be lost. Reason leaves almost everything unsettled, and so only irrational pressures can give us a stable and habitable world. Dictatorships impose their vision not so much thanks to the craven submission of their victims, but thanks to the logical inadequacy of available rational compulsion. Authority doesn't so much twist data as fill in a vacuum left behind by their feebleness.

A man must in normal or acceptable circumstances assume that the hierarchy of his society reflects the truth at least in some measure, in that those who are respected are rightly respected, and that the ranking of ideas, like the ranking of men, is all in all just. The Platonic idea that the stratification of merit of ideas, values, social ranks and ontological layers of reality all mirror and reinforce each other, itself reflects a basic technique for the maintenance of a respect for the social order. There are of course also Manichaean religions which hold the immediate world to be in the sway of the devil. There are sometimes individuals or even entire subcommunities which are deeply cynical concerning the wider society, but this is relatively rare. It is rather more agreeable to believe that on the whole the global order is just. It is certainly uncomfortable to believe the opposite, and to consider oneself caught in an evil order. Men prefer to think themselves sinners, rather than to damn the system in which they live. A sense of personal guilt seems preferable to a deep general resentment against the cosmic order. We *like* to accept the universe. Of course, some revolutionaries-by-temperament delight in thinking precisely that the current order is wicked, but such firm believers have a substitute and genuine moral order in reserve, only waiting to take over. Ultimate though not immediate reality remains gracious.

The point about an ideocratic totalitarianism is that it

vigorously completes the circle of truth, hierarchy, social merit, social reality. The dependence of the individual on the social consensus which surrounds him, the ambiguity of facts and the circularity of interpretation are all enlisted in support of the fusion of faith and social order. This is the normal social condition of mankind: it is a viable liberal Civil Society, with its separation of fact and value, and its coldly instrumental un-sacramental vision of authority, which is exceptional and whose possibility calls for special explanation. It is the ideologically as well as organizationally eccentric accountability of power and the absence of its sacralization that are historically untypical. Anthropologists are intrigued by divine kingship: it is secular kingship which really calls for explanation. Marxist totalitarianism restored a moral order in a modern or at any rate nineteenth-century idiom, and was accepted by a Russian nation thirsting all at once for deep righteousness and for modernity. Marxism was modern *and* it incarnated messianic moral fulfilment. The struggle between Westernization and moral mysticism seemed over: here was a creed deeply satisfying both needs at once.

To what extent do men really accept this kind of picture, which societies, when confident, impose on them? This is a difficult question. The average man is not a philosopher who examines his own conscience concerning the acceptability of his credo. In most cases, he is content to live within the conventions of the local faith: he goes through the motions of believing, without either doubt or active affirmation, the assumptions on which society is organized, and he relies on others to do the same. He is not necessarily cynical, he is not laughing up his sleeve: he has other things to think about. That is a relatively comfortable condition, and it satisfies most men. The astonishing ease with which entire societies change faith when the power balance changes – as for instance the English did in the sixteenth century, or the

Czechs in the twentieth – suggests that faith is not all that deep; the ease with which even utterly preposterous regimes and ideologies perpetuate themselves suggests that men are credulous, or at least not unduly critical. In the days of communal life, the question hardly arose: religion was ritual, it was danced not thought. It was the omnibus-salvation world religion which turned religion into doctrine, and made faith as distinct from practice an issue. By absolutizing affirmations, it taught men to take ideas seriously, in some measure at least. There had to be faith before there could be doubt. Serious scepticism is derivative from and indebted to consensual dogmatism. If the clerics had not protested too much, we might never have doubted.

In the days when the authority of religion was seldom challenged, did men really believe in the doctrines they could not overtly challenge? It is hard to answer this question. If they really believed in hell-fire, how could they risk so terrible a punishment for the sake of very temporary pleasures? We know they did sin and that not all sinners were unbelievers, or even subject to inner torment and fear. How could they take such risks? If I really believed in eternal hell-fire, I might well forgo the sins of the flesh: frankly, they are not worth *that* much.

The emergence of Civil Society has in effect meant the breaking of the circle between faith, power and society. The loyal citizen of a liberal Civil Society may indeed grant a kind of conditional legitimacy to the society of which he is a member, and recognize an obligation to defend it and to observe its rules, even if he tries to change them; but he is not given to sacralizing the power structure or revering the ranking of the society. He who is above him is fortunate, or has some achievement to his credit: but is no longer better or nobler. Loyalty no longer entails credulity. The criteria of truth, the criteria of social efficiency, the social hierarchy and the distribution of advantages within society – all these are not mutually linked, and the citizen can live with the clear awareness that indeed they are not linked, that the social order is not sacred, and that the sacred is not to be approached through the social. Inquiry into truth and commitment to the maintainance of social order are separated. The social can become both instrumental and optional.

A moral order, by contrast, is comforting. It is even comforting to know that others believe in it, and that one could return to faith if one chose and find companions when so doing. There are people in the West who are atheists or agnostics but find themselves emotionally ill at ease with the brazen disbelief which has become widespread within the official hierarchy of some Western denominations. Unbelievers themselves, they found it reassuring that others at least did believe, that a confident community of the faithful survives, which one could rejoin if one were so minded. It is good to know of the faith of others, and know that a bolthole is available if the anxieties of disbelief become too acute to be borne. It is annoying to discover that they do not believe either, that one may not surreptitiously hope that they might be right, and that the world offers hope after all. Similarly, I have met people in the Soviet Union, when it still existed, who privately did not believe in Marxism and were indeed highly critical both of its tenets and of the society it had engendered, but who nevertheless found themselves strangely disturbed when, during the perestroika period, the pretence of faith gradually came to be openly abandoned by all around them. It was disorienting. It is nice to know exactly what it is one does not believe, to know that others uphold it, and that one could return to the fold, were one to be freed from one's unbelief.

In the West, the transition from a social system which at least pretended to be a fully moral order, in which cosmological and moral verities blended with the realities of daily life and underwrote them, to a functional pragmatic compromise

142

where such a faith is no longer available or at least not taken seriously, was a complex and slow process. It was much aided by economic prosperity and growth. There were all kinds of continuities and ambiguities and compromises, for better or for worse. Civil Society is above all a society whose order is not sacralized, or rather is only sacralized with ambiguity, irony and nuance. (A French aristocrat who became a decorated SS officer and admired the discipline and commitment of the Nazis nevertheless reported his embarrassment at the excessive solemnity of the passing-out parade of the Charlemagne Division of the SS, held naturally in a Teutonic oak forest: in the end, he reflected, one remains French – by which he meant, not that he was a patriot, but that he retained a sense of irony.)

The social order is now instrumental, not the guardian or agent of the absolute. Still, it needs values and a sense of obligation or commitment among its members. There is a theory, which I do not accept, that secularized or semi-secularized society simply lives morally on a kind of inherited moral capital, left over from the age of faith. In fact, it lives on a certain ambiguity, a compromise between faith and its absence and the obligation of honest doubt. It needs both, and would accommodate itself ill to a full restoration of the erstwhile moral capital.

The Russian people, if Russian literature is to be believed, have a certain predilection not merely for faith, but for positive social messianism. Marxism satisfied both these dominant cravings: its scientism promised the incorporation of Russia in a prosperously materialist West, its moral utopianism promised a total consummation, a morally superior transcendence of the West. For a long time, Marxism retained much of its plausibility. There were the cynicism of Western society during the 1930s, the abandonment of the liberal façade in fascist states, the then manifest economic and moral crisis of capitalism, the victory of the Soviet

Union in the war, the material achievements which were colossal if one considers the devastation wrought by two wars, a prolonged civil war, not to mention internal purges and massacres and economic disorganization. Later came the success of the first artificial satellite, and hence the plausibility, as late as Khrushchev's time, of an eventual overtaking of the capitalist world. All this sustained the faith despite the terror, and the terror, perhaps, in a curious way confirmed the faith.

In the end, however, the secular *Umma* failed dismally. This doesn't formally prove that all other secular religions must necessarily also fail, but it does rather suggest it. Marxism was well orchestrated, its themes were not unattractive, it certainly had its chance. It is hard to say what exactly was more fatal to it — its doctrinal absolutism, or the catastrophic nature of its economic doctrines. What ideological compromise can be or will be patched up on its ruins remains to be seen.

20

FROM THE INTERSTICES OF A COMMAND-ADMIN SYSTEM

A command-administrative system is not an invention of Lenin or Stalin; it is simply the normal condition of humanity. Throughout history, human societies were (inevitably and in that sense rightly) more concerned with maintaining their internal order and their external safety than with their rate of growth. It is the liberation of economic relationships from social and political ones, not their subjugation to them, which is exceptional and requires elucidation.

So the achievement of the Bolsheviks was not the invention of an admin-command system – they might as well claim to have invented the wheel – but rather, its imposition *after* the triumph of productive society, in the name of an improvement on it which was to be, all at once, both technical and moral, and carried out in the context of an industrial-scientific society. This allowed the domination inherent in such an organization to be incomparably more thorough than would ever have been possible in earlier, pre-modern versions of the system.

They did not, of course, initially speak of an 'admin-command system': that term only came into use when the system was denounced and abjured. They spoke of 'socialism' and 'Communism', and the terms were suffused with high moral approbation. What they meant was less than fully clear, but it was understood that legally sanctioned haggling for private advantage ('the market') was *out*. Its institutional base, private control over resources, was abolished, and it was all replaced by the politically enforced priority of social, collective considerations. The social plan was to prevail over egotistic anarchy. The political tools, processes and rules which were (a) to secure the identification of the social desiderata, and (b) to enforce them, were not clearly specified. It was assumed initially that they would be benign, at least in the end. A catastrophic weakness of Marxism was the view that these institutions did not even need to be specified or created, that they would somehow emerge by spontaneous generation in conditions of classlessness and propertylessness.

The question must be repeated – was it the ideocratic absolutism as such or its Communistic content which made the system so catastrophic? The answer must be that the total socialism (in a strong sense) was indeed an essential element in the disaster. Political authoritarianisms, even totalitarianisms, which tolerate an autonomous economy, thereby unwittingly also create a Civil Society, or at least the social potential for the emergence of a Civil Society. A modern economy capable of sustained growth is so powerful that, even if temporarily denied overt political and ideological expression, it in the end deprives even an authoritarian monopolist of faith and coercion of his total power. Terror may keep such a latent Civil Society muted, but when terror ceases it is there and it can emerge. For this reason, liberalization of non-socialist dictatorships is relatively easy: the autonomous economy is a nursery of pluralism. But socialism in any strong sense makes any such nursery impossible.

The claim that the Marxist elimination of the social bases of pluralism leads to totalitarianism is by now virtually trivial and uncontentious: time has given it proof. It is an idea underlying both the overall argument of this book and the explanation of why the notion of Civil Society has had such a powerful revival. But the obverse is much less obvious, though also probably true: namely that, under modern conditions, any totalitarianism will also inevitably be Marxist.

This claim must not, of course, be taken quite literally.

The rather baroque structure or accumulation of ideas, themes and phrases known as Marxism is a relatively contingent, almost accidental hotchpotch, a fruit of the intellectual life experiences of two men. The particular cocktail of Hegelian historiosophy, the pessimism of some of the early economic commentators of the Great Transformation, of French Communism, with a late admixture of L.H. Morgan's anthropology, plus a bit of Bohemian counterculture and anarchism, and who knows how many other elements . . . it would be absurd to claim that any totalitarianism in an industrial society somehow *must* adopt just that particular witch's brew. It has happened once, probably never to reappear, though no doubt it will live on in the covens of true believers whose fidelity knows no limits.

But in another sense, there was a deep social necessity about certain really central features of Marxism: under modern conditions, no totalitarianism could be remotely complete, could possibly be total, unless it fully dominated the economy. In a society dominated by perpetual and exponential growth (where expectation of improvement can replace coercion as the ultimate basis of the social order), if the economy is left free at all, it will in the end be too powerful. In the distant past, the economy had to be socially dominated because it was so feeble: not to do so was to risk disaster. Now, it must be dominated because it is so very strong. In other words, any real, full-blooded totalitarianism in the industrial world must be Marxist, not necessarily, or perhaps ever again, in the sense of actually invoking the bizarre assembly of ideas known by that name, but because it will operate with a unified political–ideological–economic *nomenklatura*, in the manner introduced into the world 'under the banner of Marxism'. Anything less will entail the presence of rival, even if half-hidden, power centres and so undermine the prospects of real totalitarianism.

The paradox of the Soviet Union is that it was a society

which tried to set up a new social form by design from above. It failed, and having failed, the country is now condemned whether it wishes it or not likewise to create a Civil Society from above, by design *and in a hurry*.

The process by which an open, mobile, growth-oriented, modular social order emerged from the feudal or baroque-absolutist, status-oriented, anti-productive system was long, complicated and turbulent. Notionally, it meant a basic transformation of European values as well as of social organization. The new classes and ethos which emerged were fortified by deep religious faith. They also eventually learnt to suspend that faith in the public sphere, at least to the extent of recognizing the illegitimacy of its excessive intrusion in the political arena. Political obligations became effective independently of shared faith or ritual. All this took a long time, but it meant that when the new order came it had deep roots and traditions. It took pride in its ethos, and could confront with confidence that which it had replaced. The values of work and thrift were not contemptible, they were not a mere *pis aller* to pride of birth and aggressiveness.

These advantages of a new spirit seem largely absent in the attempt to produce an instant Civil Society on the ruins of the secular *Umma*. There is no new vision and probably there ought not to be, it being recognized that doubt is socially more valuable than faith. But there has been no time for the maturation of the kind of stable serene doubt which can be a basis for action rather than for moral paralysis. There has been no time to work out a custom-hallowed compromise between muted faith and well-meaning scepticism, which would seem to be one of the crucial ingredients of Civil Society.

The bourgeoisie which had once emerged from within the interstices of the feudal command-admin system had its own kind of dignity: the bourgeoisie which is being begged to crawl out from under the stones of the Communist monolith looks much less promising. Where are the Forsythe-skis and the Buddenbrookovs? Or can one only expect a lumpenbourgeoisie, recruited from opportunist apparatchiks jumping on the market-wagon, offering their inside knowl-edge and connections, spiv mafiosi emerging shiftily from previous illegality, neo-compradors and foreign investors? Can the opportunism, cynicism and demoralization accompa-nying the collapse of the old authoritarian order – not to mention the very extensive outright criminalization – engen-der that responsible ethos which may actually be a pre-condition of an effective industrial economy? A recent Moscow joke runs as follows: what is the one thing worse than socialism? Answer: that which follows socialism.

21

THE DEFINITION OF SOCIALISM

The moral intuition underlying the idea of socialism and in particular Marxism was simple: greed, acquisitiveness, competitive ownership, possession as the main symbol of human achievement and status – all this is bad. It is not merely bad, it is also perfectly avoidable: ownership and economic competitiveness are not inscribed into the nature of things or rooted in human character. On the contrary, they are incompatible with the true essence of mankind: men who endorse individual acquisitiveness and possession are alienated from their own true nature. The absolutization of greed is a law of False Consciousness imposed by a temporary and pathological social order, which tries to protect and fortify itself by such falsehood, by generalizing and treating as inherent its own distorted, historically specific vision of man: but the truth of humanity lies in spontaneous work and co-operation.

Such was Marxist doctrine. A society free of these defects will be not only more humane and morally superior, but also be more efficient, or efficient enough for human requirements. But its main merit is that it will allow men both to fulfil themselves and to be on incomparably better terms with each other. Marxism had an elaborate doctrine with historical and philosophical foundations, but all adherents of socialism in any strong sense shared this basic intuition, even if they did not endorse all the complex codification of Marxist socio–metaphysics.

Those who use the term socialism and respond to its positive emotional charge are generally committed to some cluster of ideas such as these. The emotional charge contained in the term is not an arbitrary attachment but, on the contrary, a natural and inevitable consequence of a whole set of ideas which, whether or not valid, does at any rate have some measure of plausibility and internal coherence. It is possible to believe in it if one has a strong desire to do so, and the desire was indeed there, notably among those appalled by the extremes of inequality, widespread, acute and unnecessary suffering, and the pervasive competitiveness and ruthlessness of economically free societies. This cluster of ideas then acquires great attractiveness, in as far as it and it alone seems to offer an alternative, a hope of salvation, of escape from a highly unattractive condition. Those who have a yearning for fraternity or respect human creativity rather than mere acquisition may, in the conditions engendered by individualist industrialism, find themselves impelled to embrace these ideas, and feel that otherwise they would be doomed to despair. For those susceptible to it the idea carried a kind of moral authority: it seemed to those who embraced it that it could not be understood without also being recognized as valid, as a kind of commandment.

Naturally, in this kind of state of mind they do not use the term 'socialism' as a neutral term merely designating a specific set of social arrangements. Rather, they use it as a term whose primary constituent is the notion that it is *good*. They may not know precisely what it is, but they do know that it is good. This is the fixed datum, and the other more descriptive or sociological ingredients of the idea become correspondingly less firmly entrenched. If this, that or the other constituent turns out not to be good after all, or to engender things which are clearly repellent – well then, clearly, that is not part of true socialism after all. We had made a mistake in including it, but the real definition of the term will exclude it and replace it by something else. The goodness of the idea persists, the original empirical content is modified. 'Socialism' becomes a concept with a kind of rotating empirical content – only the positive evaluative charge remains constant. The normativeness is more central to it than any empirical content.

If historical experience turns out to be different from what had been anticipated, then the descriptive content of the idea may have to be modified a bit, though not its positive evaluative charge. There simply must be something which is both contrasted to the evils in the society which we do have, something which would constitute an inversion of its values and of its hierarchy, demoting those who now self-righteously gloat over their privileges, and which would at the same time be validated not merely by promoting us – that is just incidental – but by being good. It is this kind of implicit reasoning or rather emotional reaction which is responsible for the woolliness and instability of definitions of socialism. It is difficult to define with precision that which is revered, for precision is liable to introduce contentious elements into the definition, into something which in itself is required to be immaculate and beyond contention.

However, the basic initial definition, preceding the adjustments following on disappointments, is basically simple and lucid, and of course all the better for that. It contains one simple descriptive element – the means of production pass into social ownership – and one evaluative consequence or expectation: this being so, human relations will be good. The empirical content is not endlessly volatile, it does contain at least one immovable descriptive element – and the powerful intuition that this element carries goodness with it. In the Marxist version, this expectation is an immediate corollary of the central sociological affirmation of Marxism, namely that human conflict and antagonism are the consequence of class division and of nothing else, where classes are defined as categories of people standing in different relationships to the means of production. If this is so, then in virtue of a simple and perfectly cogent logical operation it follows that by the abolition of differential relations to the means of production (i.e. classes), by placing resources under social rather than individual control, classes are automatically made to disappear and so antagonism must also vanish, and therefore human relations become harmonious. The reasoning is impeccable: it is the premisses which are open to doubt. But in Marxism, the premisses were firmly embedded in an overall philosophy of history and in a sociology of great suggestiveness and appeal, which had many true believers in their grip.

When these consequences do not manifest themselves immediately, there are of course plenty of excuses and explanations ready to hand, explanations which it must be said are also not devoid of some plausibility. The class enemy of socialism, though legally dispossessed, is still in existence, and still seeks to re-establish the old order with the aid of external allies, and will if necessary stoop to any methods, however foul, to achieve his end. The Land of the Revolution is encircled by jealous enemies, fearing the spread of the liberating ideas to their own populations. Above all, the beneficent consequences of socialism only emerge effectively at a certain level of production and, given the backwardness of the country in question, its devastation by both an international and then a civil war, that level cannot be attained immediately. Because of the menacing posture of external enemies, the attainment of the required affluence must also be delayed through the need to allocate resources and energies to preparations for defence. Socialism had its own rather extreme version of delayed satisfaction: given the siege situation and the unscrupulousness of the foes, the delay, a little temporary authoritarianism and brutality may be unavoidable . . . A revolution is no picnic, victory is not to be had without a harsh and prolonged struggle, and it would be foolish to expect anything else.

These justifications were much invoked, and they were not wholly absurd. However, by far the most important and interesting of the explanations is that of the 'perversion' of genuine socialism. It was impossible to explain the excesses of Stalin-worship and mass murder by merely specific explanations, and in any case, those denouncing these horrors were also eager to prevent their recurrence, and to further this end it was necessary not merely to excuse and explain, but also to identify and name a sin which should not be repeated. And so the notion of distortions or perversions of socialism entered the vocabulary and thought-style of socialism as a putative surrogate-explanation. A theory which claims that history obeys laws cannot easily shrug away a phenomenon of such proportions and horror. But no intra-Marxist theory of Stalinism either secured general assent or carried much conviction. Politically, it was always embarrassing to elaborate any such theory, even if a persuasive one had been found.

One perversion, however terrible, could be accommodated. In fact, the more horrible, in a way, the more conceptually digestible. The perversions of the best are the worst. It should not be altogether surprising that so luminously beautiful an ideal as socialism should be so specially revolting if perverted. And at the same time so great, so total a transformation of the human condition could hardly be expected to come without tragedy. For Marxists, violence is not and must not be the controller of history, but she is officially recognized to be its authorized midwife. Her presence at the birth pangs of a new order was only to be expected. *Perversion* and *legitimate midwife* are not strictly compatible explanations – either/or! – but emotionally, true believers were capable of somehow conflating them.

And even in its perverted and appalling form, the new order had achieved so much! It had taken a country of illiterate peasants and turned it into a country of literate industrial workers, capable of waging and winning a war against the foremost industrial power in Europe (which also, at the time of the war, effectively controlled the entire remainder of the industrial potential of continental Europe, and enjoyed the more or less willing co-operation of a very high proportion of its inhabitants); moreover, it was capable of becoming one of the world's two superpowers and even for a time of taking the lead in the exploration of space . . . Such achievements were possible even for the distorted, perverted version of socialism: how much greater will be the achievements of the purified, unperverted variant? Those achievements cannot be long in coming. This was something which Khrushchev and many of his generation believed, and Khrushchev even put a fairly close date on the achievement. The fact that the followers had been through the horrors of Stalinism and knew full well what they were did not corrode their faith. (When the date specified by Khrushchev approached, it became a bit of an in-joke in the then USSR: people would say, smilingly, that the transition from socialism to Communism was just about to take place. What in fact happened was a catastrophic collapse of the system.)

These developments did however mean that the idea of socialism had now acquired a new and different kind of internal logic. Initially, there were only two really essential elements: belief in the abolition of private property, of as it were institutionalized egoism, and in the crucial consequence, namely, human goodness and a deeply satisfying social order. Now, a third element was added in the form of a proviso: the desirable consequences do indeed follow, as we had always maintained, but only provided that no perversions/distortions intervened to rob the intended human beneficiaries of socialism of what was their due. The nature of those perversions – the 'cult of personality' – was more or less clearly identified, even if not properly incorporated in the overall theory, and so the overall notion lost little of either its lucidity or even its appeal. It had become just a little more complex in its structure. The 'perversions' were a kind of epicycle introduced *ad hoc* into the system to make it work, rather than being a natural corollary of its initial insights. But those who experienced a psychic need to respond to its appeal could still do so without blatant and overwhelming logical discomfort. The qualification contained in it made sense and even had a kind of plausibility, though it was difficult to derive it from the basic premisses of the theory. The compatibility of this modification with the central corpus of Marxist ideas was questionable, but was not questioned too much: as Marx did not say, authoritarian societies do not generally ask questions to which there is no comfortable answer.

One could schematize the logical situation as follows: if the original extension of the notion of socialism – propertylessness entailing goodness – corresponds to a circle, the present definition equated it with the extent of the circle minus one segment, which stands for the perversions such as the cult of personality. That bit – which had alas only too forcefully demonstrated its historical reality, the fact that could co-exist with the other, formal properties of socialism (no means of production left in private hands) – had to be excised from the content of the idea. As one true believer, Isaac Deutscher, put it, there was a contradiction between the socialist base of the Soviet Union and its political superstructure, and so the evil superstructure could not last. (It didn't: what he could not conceive was that it would also bring down the socialist basis with it.) The possibility of that contradiction was hard to explain in Marxist terms, but no matter: history would see to its eventual overcoming, as it could be relied on to ensure the elimination of other and earlier contradictions, and all would be well. The extension of the original idea was modified and diminished, but it still remained very considerable and even plausible.

After the fall of Khrushchev, retrospectively still much deplored in Russia by some members of his generation, who had retained the hope of making the system work without distortions – they feel that had been their last real chance –

came the Age of Stagnation, the period of Brezhnev. By the general and none too exacting standards of world history, it was not too bad a time. The number of political prisoners came to be counted in hundreds or thousands, but no longer in millions. They were selected not at random but (give or take the occasional police error or private vengeance) for genuine dissent and opposition. Literacy became near-universal, housing tolerable (90 per cent of Muscovites, for instance, living in their own rather than communally shared apartments), and living standards were quite high, in comparison with the past if not with the free world. There was no hunger. Clothing was standardized but decent. On the Moscow underground round about the 1960s, it became impossible to distinguish a worker from an intellectual by his clothing; and neither was badly dressed. Nor could you tell them apart by their reading matter: both of them read good literature, probably because trash was unobtainable.

Compared with the remembered past, this was indeed a good condition. If only the Soviet Union were an island unto itself and the outside world did not exist or could be insulated, then, most certainly, far from feeling a need to reorganize and reconstruct, the system would have joyously celebrated its own triumph. Socialism would claim the achievement of a level of affluence never known in the previous history of mankind, and at the same time even a level of liberty never locally known by such broad masses (though on occasion exceeded by very limited and privileged élites). Under the Czars, only some were free, and now many were at least a little bit free. And there was more to come, certainly of affluence, possibly of freedom.

But the Soviet Union was not an island unto itself. Far from it. On the contrary, it was locked in an ideological competition with the capitalist world, involved in a race for both economic and military preponderance, and for influence in the Third World. In Khrushchev's time, it still believed it could and would win.

By the time of the coming of perestroika, however, it had become perfectly obvious that it was unambiguously and irrevocably losing in both races. Moreover, it found itself in a cleft stick: it could diminish backwardness by allowing information flow between itself and the outside world, but this merely engendered discontent; or it could control communication and thus restrain discontent, but the lag would then only increase further. Gorbachev took the option of opening up, though certainly without a full appreciation of where the momentum of the movement would in the end take him.

But how is the concept of socialism to accommodate the Brezhnev era? It would be idle, unfair and ridiculous to pretend that this was simply a further extension of Stalinism and the cult of personality. The *nomenklatura* had stopped shooting each other, and its members were bribing each other instead. Succession to high office no longer entailed the death of the predecessor, whether natural or induced. Terror was no longer random, and the penalties it imposed were relatively restrained. Ordinary citizens who kept their mouths shut were now reasonably safe. Even if they did not keep their mouths shut, and provoked the authorities, men were liable to receive relatively humane sentences, in which the number of years in prison remained in single figures, and the sentence meant what it said (as opposed to the old system, in which a prison sentence 'without the right to communicate' was a code term for execution).

No, there is simply no question of equating this relatively benign social form, which does not compare all that badly with what mankind in general and Russians in particular had to endure in the past, with Stalinism. And yet, at the same time, there can be not the slightest question of admiring it, of identifying it with a shining ideal. It was not all that horrible, but it *was* squalid and sordid. It was not for this that martyrs had died, it was not for this that humanity had been created. Moreover – and it was this that proved its undoing, rather than its squalor – by international standards, it simply was not efficient enough. It was not capable of competing internationally, or of permanently maintaining that great-power status which the country had achieved under Stalin.

So, for one reason and another, this variant of the system was also a deformation, not a true expression of the socialist ideal, notwithstanding the fact that the first crucial condition of socialism – absence of private property – had been maintained, and the extremes of the cult of personality were now avoided. Conceptually speaking, we go back once again to that circle which stands for the basic intuition of socialism, the elimination of property rules which permit and encourage private greed and acquisitiveness. The original circle already has one dent in it: the deformation characterized by the cult of personality and the utmost excesses of arbitrary, unchecked power, and this had now been subtracted, as unworthy of inclusion in the shining ideal. Now, another segment must also be subtracted, the one corresponding to whatever it was that defined the Age of Stagnation, as officially designated. There was, one must add, no fully convincing or even plausible theory concerning why either, let alone both, deformations had occurred. The second one was not even clearly defined. To explain the occurrence of both these dents in terms of the premisses of the initial theory, while preserving the plausibility of that theory itself, was clearly beyond the ingenuity of any theorist.

The central intuition contained in the ideal of socialism was that the abolition of private control and greed would on its own lead to a satisfactory social order, one so excellent that it could even dispense with any political coercion. That idea had been modified once, by the admission that a distortion in the form of the cult of personality was possible, and had to be excluded. Now it seemed that the concept

recognized a further modification. The residue of true socialism was shrinking further. It became increasingly manifest
that what mattered was not so much its positive content
(social ownership), but the avoidance of a multiple and
moreover ill-defined, open-ended series of defects, which
appeared to accompany it quite naturally. Salvation seemed
ever more to be located in the avoidance of distortions,
rather than in the once luminous central idea of shared
ownership. Was there a limit to the number of distortions?
Was socialism as such not meant to engender goodness? It
seemed to engender a variety of opposites of goodness, and
the additional conditions which would prevent these perversions did not seem easy to identify. The salvation of mankind
no longer seemed to lie in socialism as such, but rather on the
avoidance of an extensive and ill-defined area of its distortions ... The available theory of salvation contained no
good premises for coping with all this.

What exactly was it that had defined stagnation? Lack of
candour, of democracy, of acceleration? The slogans suggested something of the kind, in as far as they suggested that
the introduction of these goodies (or reintroduction?) was
now at least being achieved. A rum business, in as far as
democracy and truth were supposed previously to be inherent in the notion of a Marxist society, so that their suddenly
acknowledged and emphasized absence, without even the
Hilfshypothese of excessive centralization and adulation of
personal power, was a bit odd.

Anyway, the new segment now also to be subtracted
from the original denotation of socialism didn't have all that
clear and coherent a definition itself. The inherently good
residue, which was to retain its authority and its political
sex-appeal, was itself correspondingly blurred. And how
many more segments is one to be asked to subtract, before
being left with the final residue which would be kosher?
The socialist ideal was beginning to look like an onion with

deformations as its leaves. Was there anything else? The existence of a kernel which would remain in the end was becoming doubtful.

Originally, the centre of gravity had lain in the basic intuition, the stress on the crucial collectivization of property, with the accompanying and built-in assumption that this would make men good and society efficient, all at once. This cluster of ideas has its own attractiveness and political authority built in: it was hardly possible to think it, in the terms used by those who proposed it, without approving it. The bowdlerized notion now available, bleeding copiously from its successive amputations, no longer had quite such a cogent, as it were ontologically guaranteed aura of its own authority. It could no longer terminate a discussion into which it was introduced, simply by virtue of its internal, inherent authority. Once upon a time, audiences of the right persuasion knew that a socialist policy was *ipso facto* good, even when they didn't know what the devil it was. Now this automatic *carte blanche* endorsement had lost its power.

The burden of definition and vindication now shifts away from the uncritical contemplation of those simple characteristics attributed to the kernel, and their automatically accompanying beneficent social consequences: it shifts rather to the problem of just how the deformations are to be defined, identified and evaded. Not an easy question to answer, given that they seem to be numerous, manifold and ill-defined, and that they keep turning up.

There had by now been quite a few Marxist regimes, in all kinds of climes, in countries with all kinds of previous history, and in all kinds of international contexts. The sheer variety of these contexts made deformation much harder to explain than it had been when socialism was practised in one country, which indisputably had a tragic history and found itself in exceedingly difficult circumstances. Marxist regimes existed in developed countries and in backward ones; in poly-ethnic ones and in culturally homogeneous ones; in lands endowed with democratic traditions and in those haunted by authoritarianism; in Catholic, Protestant, Orthodox Sunni, Shi'ite, Buddhist, Confucian and shamanist countries; some in Europe and some in the Third World; some had suffered colonialism and some had not, and some had practised it themselves; some in places where Marxism was established by a local struggle and some in places where it had been brought by the Red Army. Some were subservient to Moscow and some proudly and insolently independent, and even locked in conflict with the Homeland of Revolution. *All* possible combinations seem to have been tried out in the course of an exceptionally thorough controlled experiment kindly arranged by history, and the verdict seemed much the same: Marxist societies ranged from the repulsive to the unspeakable.

By the time the definition and vindication had to enumerate or define a whole long and perhaps open list of deformations, all of which have to be avoided before the residual nuclear ideal emerges and is operative in all its beauty and effectiveness, the game was given away. The idea of Marxism could now only work if endowed with a theory of deformations, and it was hardly able to produce one without making itself ridiculous. Definitions were endless, but they occurred under so many diverse conditions that no explanation was available. The game was abandoned, and remaining Western idealists were counselled to look at 'real socialism' – i.e. as actually practised in Marxist societies – with the argument that even if a bit defective (who would dispute that?) at any rate it had the advantage of existing in the real world and not just in a romantic imagination, and was at least known to be compatible with the social constraints operative in the world. And so it was: but, by the consumerist standards internationally prevalent and accepted during the latter part of the twentieth century, it was, though evidently practicable, also grossly inferior in terms of effectiveness. And this, at any rate in Europe and the ex–USSR, finally brought it down.

So, by the time the appeal has to be located not in the elusive kernel, but in the absence of that open-ended, evidently interminable series of deformations, the centre of attention shifts from the kernel to the elimination of those generic deformations, which seem to haunt so persistently that ideal essence which they also mar, but whose emanation they nevertheless seem to be. The deformation turns out to be the essence. And just this is, of course, our central theme: if there is a brief way of defining the real social content of the newly rediscovered social ideal of Civil Society, if there is a succinct manner of explaining its suddenly reacquired political suggestiveness and attractiveness, it is to be found precisely in this area. Civil Society has become the slogan or the idea which intuitively sums up all those social characteristics which normally prevent the emergence of the generic deformations, deformations which in fact appear to be, not avoidable mistakes, but something inherent in the central idea itself.

It is the combination of the pursuit of virtue and industrialism which seems to be so disastrous. Marxist societies are ideocracies, i.e. regimes not content with performing a social function at least cost, but concerned with the implementation of a moral order, the prevalence of virtue on earth. Politics becomes the imposition of righteousness. But an industrial society is by definition one in which economic activity is pervasive and crucial. To subject it to virtue, to pretend that haggling is inappropriate and immoral, and inequality is inherently improper, is to subject it to constraints which are incompatible with it. The result is the erection of an entirely spurious façade, and squalor and cynicism underneath. The unification of the economy in one single organization and its fusion with the political and ideological hierarchy is not merely most inefficient: it also inevitably leads to both totalitarianism and humbug. In an industrial society, full socialism cannot but be totalitarian – and totalitarianism cannot but be socialist. To allow an independent economic zone is to leave an enormous breach in the authoritarian system, given the importance of the economy. To deprive Civil Society of an independent economic base is to throttle it, given the inevitability of political centralization.

22

A NEW POSITIVE DEFINITION

The simplest definition of socialism, which contented itself with looking at the actual social reality and refrained from evaluation, would run as follows: socialism is the command-administrative manner of running an industrial society.

Those who retain some measure of loyalty to the habit of endowing socialism with a positive emotive charge will of course resent such a definition, as it would seem to them deliberately and in their view unjustly endowed with a negative emotive charge. The command–administrative system is the last in the series of excuses/explanations of what it was that had gone wrong with the implementation of socialism. There is, apparently, some other way of running socialism, other than by the command–admin method, though it is not clear what that could be ('market socialism' or 'socialist market' is spoken of, though it is not clear what this can mean over and above an obfuscation of issues).

Here one must return to some basics. When two or more men are involved in some activity which includes the distribution of tasks, of responsibilities, of reward, of control over resources or produce, there are a number of ways in which the precise pattern of co-operation can be determined:

1) They can haggle with each other until they agree, each independently controlling some resources. This is known as the market.

2) There can be an authority structure such that one of them can in the end simply decide who does what, who gets what, etc. This is the command-admin system.

3) They can 'give' each other resources and output, and do for each other, without too much haggling or commanding. One variant of this possibility, fairly well explored by

anthropologists, arises when custom prescribes the seeming unconstrained co-operation, division of labour, and so on.

4) Men may perhaps 'genuinely' give and co-operate without domination by custom, inspired by pure love and unconstrained co-operativeness. Presumably this may become possible in conditions of very advanced and generalized affluence, when scarcity makes men nonchalant about who has what, and when also human nature is transformed sufficiently for them not to quarrel about positional goods, i.e. the kind of relative advantage which must in the nature of things remain scarce even in conditions of great material prosperity.

There would seem to be no other way of arranging the co-operating of men and the distribution of goods among them. One can begin by dismissing (4) as unrealistic, certainly for the time being, probably for ever. We have not reached that level of affluence, certainly not on a global scale, and there is no evidence whatever under any social system of the kind of transformation of human nature which would lead to spontaneous co-operation. Likewise, we can dismiss (3). It is not unrealistic in itself, and no doubt can and does operate in small, intimate and fairly stable communities. In fact, the charm of such communities lies precisely in the fact that this is feasible among them, and more than feasible, that it is often preferred and more effective.

That, in effect, leaves two and only two ways of running human societies. (The two methods can of course be mixed with each other.) Let us take the command system first.

The method in itself is relatively neutral. Perhaps it is inherently bad to the extent that it would be best of all if no one ever issued any commands to anyone. This at any rate is the central moral intuition of anarchists. But it is virtually impossible to imagine the running of a complex industrial society, such as is presupposed by the standard of living to which we have become accustomed, without the use of definite instructions which are carried out and which are enforced by sanctions. In Marxism this is somewhat obscured by the doctrine which anticipates the replacement of the government of men by the administration of things, but the administration of things cannot but incorporate some measure of instruction to the men who administer the said 'things'.

What clearly matters is whether the system is plural: are there ways of checking on those who have the power to command, and is the power limited in time and area, and so on? A command system in which those who exercise command are subject to rules, where the sanctions underwriting their commands are limited and humane, where the authority to command rotates and is allocated in the light of suitability, and so on – such a command system may not be too bad, or in any case may be the best that we can have.

One way of defining Civil Society is simply as the formula which attempts to sum up the devices which humanize the admin–command element in society, whose sheer presence in some measure is inevitable. What turned the notion of admin–command into a pejorative one was of course the fact that it was unique, centralized, un–plural, ideocratized (by including the ideological function, and practising it in an absolutist spirit, crediting itself with total rectitude).

All of which leaves us the question of the relative place of commanding and haggling. If enterprises are genuinely independent, we simply have market capitalism under a new name: the independent units control their own resources and so engender inequality of wealth. Alternatively, if their independence is limited, a real concern of participants cannot but be with power in the (possibly camouflaged) command status system, and we simply have a new variant of a bureaucratic centralism. The hybrid and obscure notion of 'socialist market' has little to commend it. Either productive units do have genuine autonomy (in which case they behave as in the market), or they do not. Cosmetic internal democracy of enterprises does not affect the matter. It may of course have some merit: genuine or theatrical participation may be effective, or good for morale. On the other hand, genuine creativity, as in the arts, sciences or scholarship, is often strictly incompatible with committee management: one creative person must be in charge. If some mixed entrepreneurial socialism were feasible, one must assume that the erstwhile Yugoslavs, who tried ardently to find it for decades, ever since their in-between international position gave them a strong motive for seeking to be the pioneers of the Third Way, would have found it. No doubt hybrid enterprises can function in some cases – but this is not some kind of general solution, but rather an attempt to protect the residual piety of those who have elevated the word 'socialism' to sacred status, and crave its retention in the pantheon of values even after the events of the penultimate decade of the twentieth century.

While the hybridization of individual enterprises probably does not make much sense in general, the hybridization of society as a whole does make a great deal of sense. The unfortunate consequence of the collapse of the Marxist *Umma* is that it seems to some people, quite incorrectly, to constitute a vindication of the complete marketization of society, a reinforcement of the minimal state and maximal market doctrine. This is most unfortunate, though it is perfectly possible that a sensible mixed economy may be run under the cover of hyper-liberal imagery and slogans, on the tacit principle that of course you can have a mixed economy and intimate co-operation between industry and political authority, provided you call it strict monetarism.

Throughout human history, societies have had to give priority to considerations of maintenance of order and security over considerations of enhancement of production. In any case, they seldom had the latter option. In other words, political and religious organization on the whole dominated purely economic elements. Once only did the balance change definitively, under exceedingly favourable circumstances – eighteenth-century England had a fine social infrastructure, a balance of power in its polity, and so the market could be given its head. The technology was just about powerful enough for that, and yet blessedly feeble enough not to destroy society or its environment, or give anyone power to dominate society militarily.

All that has changed, and will never happen again. Modern technology is enormously powerful, and contains a disastrous potential for ecology and for the possibility of terrorism, by generating devastating weapons controllable by a small number of persons. At the same time, the bulky, package-deal quality of the social infrastructure makes it imperative that a very large proportion of the total output, something in the neighbourhood of one half, passes through the hands of political institutions. The atomization of society means that morally unacceptable destitution for the weak cannot be prevented by families or social sub-units, but only by relatively central institutions. The successful economies seem to be those in which effectively autonomous productive units co-operate informally but intimately with the polity. In a society in which the centre controls the deployment of half the output, and in any case creates and controls the social and economic climate and the environment, all trading is in effect insider trading. This is and will remain an insider-trading society, pretences and legal fictions to the contrary notwithstanding.

So, in the past, political considerations trumped economic ones and the economic side of life simply could not be granted full autonomy – in other words, a market society was impossible – because the economy was so pathetically feeble. The avoidance of starvation had to be – and could only be – assured politically, if indeed it could be assured at all. A liberation of the market from political control would have been catastrophic. In the future, a real market economy will be impossible for precisely the opposite reason – because the economy is so appallingly powerful. The side-effects of economic operations, if unrestrained, would disrupt everything – the environment, the cultural heritage, human relations. They simply have to be politically restrained, though the control may be – and probably should be – camouflaged, consensual, negotiated and subtle. The economy must be free enough to provide plural institutions with their bases, but not powerful enough to destroy our world.

For all these reasons, industrial society is bound to be and remain a mixed economy, though it may well use quite different ideological folklore for its public relations and self-image. But the institutional devices which make its command element humane are the pluralism contained in the notion of Civil Society, and its pre-conditions contain the need for a plural productive system. If socialism means that political constraints are put on the economy, then virtually all, or perhaps *all* societies without qualification, are socialist. The mistake of socialism as a salvation-faith was the supposition that the specific nature of that social control was somehow self-evident, and would make its unique nature manifest as soon as private control was abolished, and that the more complete that collective control, the better. Nothing is further from the truth. Messianic socialism, which equated control of the economy with salvation, had to learn this the hard way: it was forced to seek a theory of deformations. It was not really capable of developing one. Better begin at the other end, and try to find a benign form of political control in the sea of malignant ones (distortions). It might be that political control balanced by an autonomous set of production units provides the answer – that Civil Society *is* the solution.

There are endless forms of social control, many or most of them repulsive. Merit or demerit attaches to the *kind* of control, not to its nature. And it must not be so complete or so extreme as to make it impossible for the economy to sustain countervailing forces to the state. In a sense, it is still true that 'we are all socialists now': for the question is not *whether*, but *what kind* of socialism (i.e. political control over production) there is to be, how complete, and how it in turn is checked. And the answer is bound to be that the control must be such as to avoid ecological disaster, or destitution for some, or the possibility of blackmail; but, these aims being ensured, the control should be far less than complete.

23

TOWARDS A DESIRABLE UNHOLY ALLIANCE

The age of parity between two world systems, which stretched from 1945 or the Soviet acquisition of nuclear weapons till the late 1980s, had some distinctive and marked features. It was a period of world peace based on, as the phrase went, Mutually Assured Destruction.

Without the nuclear threat, there would unquestionably have been a Third World War: there was a number of crises in which both sides would under normal circumstances have felt convinced that they could not possibly back down without irrevocably losing face and thereby weakening their own position irretrievably. The fear of such a humiliation and its consequences, and the hope of victory even if at some considerable cost, would have impelled each side to take a stand, and, given the fact that the other side would feel exactly the same and that the two stands were mutually incompatible, war would have broken out.

Nuclear weapons, however, changed all that. Both sides knew that this time there would be no victors and that the cost of war would be far greater than anything that could be gained by it. Threatening a war still made sense, but waging it did not. Whether one can credibly threaten something which also involves one's own suicide is a good question, which was indeed frequently asked. The evidence rather suggests that one can. In any case, the nuclear balance of power did work, and overall peace was preserved. Wars were only fought by proxy, in the Third World.

The world system which this engendered was curious. Outright war was now impossible, or at any rate was overwhelmingly against the interests of those capable of waging it alone, and so it was not waged. But war by proxy was perfectly feasible, and did occur fairly often. And it turned out that in these wars, at any rate if fought in difficult (mountain, jungle) terrain, technology did not count for so very much after all, or at least was not decisive, whereas determination, capacity to sustain hardship, brutal willingness to impose it on foe and friend, ruthless organization and discipline and conviction, counted for a great deal more. Marxism may have failed to be the Calvinism of Collective and Emulative Economic Growth (as I once, long ago, thought it might be), but it did prove itself in China and South-east Asia to be the new Prussian drill sergeant. Twice in Indo-China and once each in Algeria and Afghanistan (though in the latter cases of course without benefit of Marxist ideology), technologically superior forces of a developed country were eventually defeated by local organizations, or were at least exhausted and induced to withdraw, partly owing to international and internal public opinion. Their opponents were sustained with supplies and diplomatically by members of the rival world camp. The lesson was well learnt, and the period saw the termination of colonial, 'overseas' empires, notwithstanding the fact that the military balance of power continued to favour advanced technology (as shown by the Falkland and Gulf wars), or indeed to favour it more than ever before. The timidity of intervention in erstwhile Yugoslavia shows how deeply the lesson was learnt.

With the temporary Soviet–American alliance or collusion which followed perestroika, this system for whatever it was worth came to an end. We are perhaps facing the emergence of a new kind of international order, though we do not yet know what it will be. Certain possibilities however have been highlighted by the Gulf War.

There is one new factor in the situation: the direction of the development of military technology. The details are specialized and technical: but of the overall trend there can be little doubt. Weapon systems of appalling and sometimes uncontrollable destructiveness are becoming cheaper, smaller, more open to disguise, easier to erect, manipulate and deploy. As yet they are not universally and easily accessible: only societies endowed with fairly sophisticated industrial systems, a competent scientific intelligentsia, an adequate demographic and financial base can at present acquire and effectively deploy these horrible weapons. Nevertheless, the general trend is clear: the time is not too far away when dreadful weapons of mass destruction or contamination will become accessible to far too many people, to all kinds of governments and non-governmental political groups, some willing to use them for purposes of blackmail and terrorism. We cannot be sure just how soon these weapons will be very easy to acquire and deploy, but such a time cannot be too far distant. The direction of the curve of this technological development is obvious and there for all to see.

The political consequences of this are also obvious. Sooner or later, quite possibly sooner, some group will be in possession of a capacity to threaten, say, the release of an incurable epidemic, or a general poison, or something engendering a chain reaction. The group in question can use this capability to blackmail the rest of mankind, either for its own advantage, or in the fanatical pursuit of some ideological goal. The rest of mankind will then face the options of surrender or destruction, and as the situation may well occur repeatedly, in the end collective destruction becomes inevitable. During the cold war, we were fortunate in that the capacity of Mutually Assured Destruction was only in the hands of two relatively rational, restrained and realistic powers. Though one of them was an ideocracy which was assured by its faith that its own victory was inevitable, in practice both sides were inspired by pragmatic caution. We cannot expect to remain so lucky for ever. Only the establishment of a world authority endowed with the means and the will to prevent any group from acquiring the capability for such blackmail can ensure human survival.

It is quite easy to preach the desirability of world government, and somewhat less easy to indicate realistic methods by which this end is to be attained. It is easy to suspect that some really dreadful nuclear war will have to happen first, before the political will is generated for creating the central authority which would prevent the recurrence of the disaster. Nevertheless, the kind of World International which crystallized during the approach period to the Gulf War gives some hope – it would be wrong to put this in any stronger terms – that the institutionalization of adequate control to prevent generally disastrous wars may not be so very far away. In other words: there is at present not merely the need for world central authority, but also a realistic social base for its emergence.

For the sake of simplicity – simplifications don't undermine the argument – let us assume there are two kinds of polity in the world, industrially developed ones and underdeveloped ones. Take the second category first.

The regimes of what used to be called the Third World vary a good deal, but contain a significant proportion of exceedingly nasty ones. The reason for this is not hard to find. Authorities in a pre-industrial polity can easily buy or receive, in the form of 'aid' from their patron-state, military and police equipment, which enables them to control the society in question without too much difficulty. Local resources are no match for those provided as aid to the client-state. For reasons which have operated throughout human history, the power-holders in such a polity have little real interest in promoting 'development'. Their own perks depend on their monopoly of power within the society, and not on the productivity of the society as a whole. Repellent Third World regimes often resemble most pre-industrial polities, which were oppressive, brutal and exploitative. The only difference is that these contemporary versions can and do borrow coercive equipment of a more developed kind, and use it to lord over a society which is technologically backward. The disproportion of power is thus greater than ever and tilted in favour of the authorities as long as they preserve the monopoly of comprador coercion.

Though these nasty little dictatorships do exist in the Third World, it is interesting that on the whole they are not very warlike, and not much of a menace to their neighbours or to world peace. This, once again, is not accidental, but follows from the logic of the situation. War is an unpredictable and, in the main, a zero-sum game (or worse). The average prospects of two combatant units cannot be *ex hypothesi* better than even: they can't both win, though they can both lose. The Prince of a petty dictatorship finds himself in the position which Machiavelli described for his Italian Renaissance predecessor: he is in a no-win situation, for if his generals win the battle against the enemy they turn against him, and if they lose or look like losing they run away. Given the low level of loyalty both on the part of officers and populations, war is exceedingly risky, and the odds of a successful outcome for the little dictator are far less than even. Moreover, being dictator of two little principalities rather than one is not such a great improvement, and most certainly the difference is not remotely as great as that between being a dictator in one place only and not being one at all, even assuming one gets away before being captured and punished by the successor regime. There can be no doubt about the correct strategy: the armed forces are there to be used against internal opposition, and external conflict is to be avoided as much as possible. Possible gains are improbable, losses are probable and disastrous.

The behaviour of small dictatorships in the underdeveloped world has in the main been in accordance with the logic of this argument. The decolonized world has seen some wars but not all that many, and far fewer than one might have expected. Such wars as did occur were frequently not genuine local conflicts, but by proxy expressions of wider confrontation, in which the local combatants were merely acting under instruction or at least with strong encouragement from their block-patrons. On the whole the local dictators have, sensibly enough from their own viewpoint, used their often exiguous resources to ensure themselves adequate means for internal domination and have limited their external ambitions, and profited from the fact that their neighbours were restrained by similar, parallel considerations. One particularly nasty little dictator who proclaimed himself Emperor and used Napoleonic symbolism nevertheless conspicuously refrained from any attempts at Napoleonic expansionism. The disproportion in power between the purchased, imported means of coercion and what can locally be created in opposition is so great that the cards are heavily stacked in favour of the state apparatus and against internal opposition. (Palace revolutions from within the *apparat* have much better prospects and do occur.) So the overall situation favours political domination and economic stagnation.

All in all the Third World did not reproduce the near-continuous and virtually ritualized warfare characteristic of feudalism or of some tribal societies. One may hazard the guess that the warfare-addiction of feudal barons is connected with the superiority of defence over attack: just because each baron is relatively safe within his own keep, they can all afford the luxury, exercise, diversion and status-reinforcement involved in occasional raids against each other's strongholds. After the harvest is safely in, two neighbouring tribes can indulge in the annual ritual battle in which there is much joyous shooting and at the end of which the score resembles one of those careful First Division football matches where both teams employ a defensive strategy, and where the score will be something like 2 − 1. It is then all added to the long-term inter-tribal tally so that over time it all evens out. Modern weapons, even of the cheaper variety, are however a little too potent for such cosy forms of violence, and their possessors in the underdeveloped world tend to restrict their use to the serious and essential business of keeping themselves in power against their internal rivals, rather than wasting them on the relative luxury of inevitably risky external adventure.

So, is the fear of really terrifying, blackmail-potential weapons falling into irresponsible hands a chimera? Not so.

First consider the developed world, meaning those societies capable of producing the most potent weapons largely or wholly from their own resources and without external aid. If a major power satisfying this characterization chooses to blackmail the rest of the world − either submit or let us all perish together − there is in the nature of the case *nothing that can be done about it*. It is pointless to discuss in this context the deep and interesting moral question whether in such a situation it would be better to submit or to resist. What is interesting and relevant in this context is that − good news does occasionally come one's way − for the present at least it does not look probable that any major power would indeed act in this way.

This is quite different from the situation earlier in this century, when there were major powers in the developed world which almost certainly would have indulged in this blackmail, had they been able to. At present it no longer looks as if this particular terrible menace is imminent. It may of course always come back and we cannot provide guarantees of its future absence, but just now this horror at least does not seem to be on our horizon. Why are we so fortunate?

The answer is very relevant to our main theme because it

can be summed up as follows: the major powers and the societies over which they preside, though they may not put it in that way, have become converted to the values and assumptions associated with the idea of Civil Society. They no longer consider honour and military glory to be values in themselves; not only do they not think or feel like warrior aristocrats, they do not think like peasants either – they clearly do not equate wealth with acreage. They value output, which they know to be unrelated to military strength (or even to be inversely related to it) and to territory, or even to direct control of natural resources. They favour institutional, economic and political pluralism, and a compromise ideology which does not absolutize itself or sacralize the society. So they will not go to war for the faith, any more than they will for either land, honour or glory. This is the general tenor of the powerful, developed countries. Some of them have evolved towards that position over centuries; some were converted to it by military defeat, followed by brilliant economic victory, after 1945; and one group of societies was converted to it by striking and decisive defeat in the economic inter-ideological race in the post-1945 world, a race whose outcome became plain for all to see by the late 1980s.

Nineteen eighty-nine may go down in history as the culmination of the victory of productive over rival values. Nineteen forty-five saw the victory of producers over those clinging to an industrial variant of honour and land values; 1989, the victory of interest over an industrial variant of faith and salvation, of making virtue the concern of the state. The cold war turned out to be one of the most clearly decisive wars in history: one side collapsed ignominiously and openly admitted defeat, and proclaimed for all the world to hear that its gods were false gods, its past a total and shameful mistake. Yet the cold war remained a *cold* war! Contrary to the normal logic of conflict, the losing side did not reach deeper into the armoury and did not – as it well might have done – threaten to impose shared suicide, by turning the conflict into a violent one. Economic victory was sufficient and induced the loser, whose military potential remained intact and was exceedingly formidable, to capitulate. Perhaps this was the first time in history when a purely economic battle, not confirmed even for the sake of form or honour on any battlefield, was totally decisive. Good chess players do not insult their opponents by playing on in lost situations: they resign. The Soviet leadership did not behave like either a vindictive loser or an honour-bound samurai and fight on: it resigned. Perhaps the cult of chess in the ex-USSR had a little beneficial influence . . .

But of course there are, within this camp of the defeated in the ideological race, not merely one but two great powers. Their reaction to the defeat is somewhat different. After some not surprising vacillations by the leadership, the Russians have opted for a lurch towards liberalization, in the hope (somewhat problematic) that this will bring economic improvement in its train, or at least will make it possible. While intellectual liberalization was unquestionably achieved, economic success was not, and economic failure continues to endanger the entire experiment.

By contrast, the Chinese leadership, while experimenting effectively and apparently not without success with economic liberalization, has firmly and resolutely stood out against political liberalization, and has not hesitated to use force and face the loss of life incurred in the pursuit of this policy. It has opted for an ideologically opportunist development dictatorship which, in the interests of stability, perpetuates the political organization and discipline and nominally the ideology of Marxist totalitarianism. But it is doubtful whether the Chinese now take the ideology seriously: they are presumably influenced by the consideration that tinkering with the system and its ideological pillar can be catastrophic – as the Russian experience has indicated.

There is of course no shadow of doubt concerning which of these two attitudes is morally more attractive: the passionate striving for a free life, combined with economic ineptitude, which characterizes the Russians and which is reflected in perestroika and its sequel, is deeply endearing. No country has had a history more haunted by authoritarianism and brutality than Russia; no country has a literature which so passionately expresses a striving for contrary values. The folly of liberalization expresses this aspect of Russia. The cold Chinese calculation that economic improvement must come first and that political changes (if they are to come at all) must wait, is not something which warms one's heart. The sad thing is that, alas, it may well be the correct strategy: a prosperous and visibly growing country can eventually liberalize with impunity, whereas liberalization in a period of economic deterioration and crisis will in the end be self-defeating, and may well lead to some new kind of dictatorship. It is too soon to tell, and one may only hope that one's pessimistic fears will prove to be unjustified; but it would be wrong to misrepresent the situation.

However, from the viewpoint of the present issue – Civil Society and the international world order – it is relevant that neither of the two erstwhile great homelands of the revolution is really opposed to the ideal of Civil Society. The ex-Soviet Union has overtly embraced it, though in the post-putsch period after August 1991 it looks to be on the verge of disintegration and economic collapse. This cannot be said of China. The stance of its leaders is not appealing, but it is not obvious that they would necessarily be hostile to a tacit, or even non-tacit, world condominium based on an alliance of the industrial great powers determined to prevent some kind of military blackmail from wherever it may come, but otherwise administering the world loosely speaking in terms of Civil Society conventions.

If the great industrial powers seem to be oriented in this

direction, and petty dictatorships in the main constitute no menace, where is the danger? The events leading up to the Gulf War made this plain.

There are regimes which possess a technological-industrial base large enough to acquire in due course a really menacing blackmail potential, and which also possess a demographic and social base large enough for such an aim. Iraq clearly was and is such a country.

Motivation? There are two possibilities (which are not mutually exclusive, and they might be superimposed on each other): the leader of such a country might be deeply rooted in one of those patronage-based political systems in which winner always takes all, and in which mercy to opponents, or any restraint when one has power in one's hands, is simple folly and is deeply despised. It is also unlikely to elicit similar restraint on the other side, and thus is only conducive to the self-destruction of anyone who displays it. The leader in question may be deeply imbued with the political machismo which normally constitutes the culture of such polities. Such, after all, was the political culture of most agrarian societies. Alternatively, the society in question might be an *Umma*, a charismatic community sincerely and totally committed, or whose leaders are committed, to the absolute validity of its religious vision, and the moral obligation to impose it whenever it possesses the might. Muslim law formally obliges Muslim rulers to wage the Holy War for the extension of the faith every ten years at the very least – ten years being the maximum time allowed for truce with the infidel – *if* conditions are propitious and victory reasonably likely. Who knows when, given the unforeseeable potentials of modern technology, that crucial final condition may not seem to be fulfilled? Some of them quietly ignore this obligation and will continue to do so. Some might not.

The basic logic of the Gulf War was not that Saddam had

broken international law, but that he was very close to acquiring a position (notably if he succeeded in controlling the entire Gulf oil-producing area) in which he would be in a position to blackmail the world, especially if his control of the oil zone were combined with the capacity to deliver a nuclear warhead even at distant enemies. We did not seem too far removed from all this. What made the partial destruction of his war machine possible was the very recent conversion of the world dual system, from one in which two rivals did not allow the other to impose his will on Third World countries, quite irrespective of the merits of any specific conflict, to a new one in which at the top of the industrial-technical league there is an alliance of polities either embracing or eager eventually to embrace the values of Civil Society. It is unlikely that this alliance will initiate a crusade in the name of Civil Society, and impose it throughout the world in some newly rediscovered missionary zeal. It is however possible – and we have had an informal dress rehearsal for it – that a type of world condominium will arise, which will content itself with destroying potential blackmailers.

The significance of the Gulf War may in fact turn out to be that it was the first step in establishing a kind of precedent or case law for precisely this type of limited but functional and realistic world government. The informal International of Consumerist Unbelievers, societies no longer committed either to Honour and Land or to a Total Faith, but only to a pragmatic and pluralist pursuit of wealth, did not institutionalize itself as a permanent un-Holy Alliance of conservative peace-keepers, nor did anyone codify the underlying logic of the alliance. This may be a pity, but it may perhaps be remedied in the future.

24

DEMOCRACY OR CIVIL SOCIETY

The transformation of Eastern Europe which began in 1985 and reached its culmination in 1989 and after the abortive coup of August 1991 in Moscow is sometimes referred to as the process of 'democratization'. Is this word, rather than 'Civil Society', to be preferred?

Not too much hinges on the choice of a mere word perhaps, but all in all it would seem that 'Civil Society' is greatly preferable. The defect of 'democracy' is the naïvety of the model which it suggests, and which it encourages its users to take seriously. The underlying model is that of a society which is a fruit of the will of its participants or members. It is a view which would make society sound if indeed it expresses, reflects or implements the will of its members, but pathological if that will is overruled by some means or other.

This, of course, also constitutes the source of the appeal of the term: the theory built into it answers the problem of validation. In a world in which the faith in the transcendent foundation of values is absent, human will seems a natural, plausible, perhaps indeed the only eligible heir. What else could possibly justify social arrangements other than our consent? 'Democracy' could then seem to be the name of the only plausible base for social authority. Democracy appears as the only possible source of political legitimacy in a secularized, naturalized world.

An awkward question then arises: can it also without blatant circularity and prejudgement of issues validate the transition *from* a world imbued with transcendent faith and the obligations implicit in it, a world in which human will is not sovereign but where righteousness consists in submission to a higher will, *to* a world which has shed or is shedding such conviction or refrains from taking it seriously, and is therefore thrown back on human will? That transition cannot itself be validated by 'human will' without circularity or prejudgement. Each such world validates itself and enjoys the endorsement of its citizens: and no third one exists which would choose between them.

Normally, of course, societies and their arrangements are not and indeed cannot be chosen by the will of their members at all. Men are born into and live within the institutions and culture of their society, which they often take for granted, roughly in the manner in which they speak prose. They are made by the culture they live in, and do not come to it fully formed and able to 'choose' a society which pleases them. A culture is a system of prejudgement. Social institutions and cultures are seldom chosen: they are our fate, not our choice.

The normative model suggested by the notion of democracy has precisely these somewhat misleading associations. It suggests men who are simultaneously pre-social and yet fully made, capable of assessing social options from the outside. Of course, men do indeed sometimes dislike the way things are going in the community in which they live, and in a certain negative way democracy can be said to be absent when the rejection of the current state of affairs by the members is overruled or ignored. But generally speaking, the democratic model ignores the fact that institutions and cultures *precede* decisions rather than *follow* them. Or rather, this is true of major fundamental alternatives. Democracy, like the market (whose ideological appeal has a similar logic), may be an excellent manner of making relatively minor choices within an overall settled structure, but it cannot without circularity and absurdity be granted the capacity to choose between total social structures or value-systems. Or rather: *some* pre-existing structures contain within themselves a 'democratic' way of settling minor issues. The inapplicability of the democratic model to major issues is not a technical, but a *logical* point. It is not that major issues are less well handled by this method; rather, it simply makes no sense to think of them so handled. Our culture gives us our identity: so *who exactly* is to choose a culture, when there is as yet no self, no identity, no vision or set of values, which would carry out the choice?

The *Mayflower* model, applicable to the situation in which a group of intellectually serious, self-conscious and lucid ideological migrants actually discuss and draw up the social contract for a community which they are about to establish, is unusual, though it does sometimes occur. But even, or especially, when this happens, it can happen precisely because moral consensus between the members of this kind of community already exists. It precedes, rather than is created by, a collective act of will. It is possible just because a culture has already in effect formed the constituent assembly of a new society, and has given its members the will and concepts for so doing. Far from being pre-social raw human material, the Pilgrims were morally fully formed. It was precisely that which blessed their enterprise with success.

The naïve formulations of the democratic ideal detach it from its institutional and cultural conditions, and tend implicitly to suggest that it is something valid for humanity as such. It is, in fact, eminently doubtful whether democracy is in some way rooted in human nature. Man is indeed a social animal, and needs community; communities, if they are to survive, generally need a system of social roles and positions. These are by no means always (or in the majority of cases) egalitarian, and they do not generally give all members of the community equal weight in the making of decisions. Societies and communities are endowed with a role structure, and in most circumstances this is, for better or worse, not democratic. We may deplore this, but it is a fact. Society maketh men, but men do not generally choose their society. Neither the *choice* nor the *equality* implied by the notion of 'democracy' is inherent in the human soul or social condition.

While democracy is not inherent in human nature, it does have some kind of affinity with the condition in which we find ourselves. A society committed to growth and hence to occupational instability is thereby also committed to a basic egalitarianism: it is debarred from using a device otherwise very widespread among societies, namely the permanent and enforced division of the members of society into sharply separated categories of people with distinct rights and duties, who also deeply internalize their status as members of this or that category. This device, which is normally a great help to the functioning of societies by endowing them with stability and encouraging acceptance by men of their lot, is precluded among us, or if its use is attempted leads to great stresses and tensions. The one open and brazen effort to set up a caste system under modern conditions, South African apartheid, failed conspicuously.

Again, it is not easy for this kind of society to be an *Umma*, an ideocracy. A society tied to an expanding technology and hence to an expanding cognitive base cannot absolutize or freeze its perception of the world. Such a society acquires a sense of the independence of natural truth from society and its requirements, and it is difficult for it really to take seriously the notion of a definitive and final revelation. Its sophistication concerning alternative conceptualizations of the same material, and its sense of the separability of issues, makes it difficult or impossible to adopt a vision which carries in itself an authoritative assignment of rights and duties, and the vindication of such attributions. The idea of the Management of the universe practising cognitive favouritism and nepotism among its own creation – which is what the idea of Revelation means – is morally repugnant in a society whose tacit entrenched constitution proclaims

equal and symmetrical access to truth. A measure of secularization, or at any rate a compromise between serious inquiry
and ritual formulae, is required within it. A secular version
of Revelation offered by Marxism fared even worse than
traditional, overtly transcendental religions. It collapsed with
a speed and completeness which is quite unprecedented in
the intellectual history of mankind, and unlike religions in
the literal sense appears to have left virtually no nostalgia in
the souls of those who had been so systematically and
pervasively subjected to it. 'Once a Catholic . . .' is not
echoed by 'Once a Communist . . .'. Quite the reverse: ex-
Bolsheviks make the most passionate and committed bolsho-
phobes. The Bolsheviks did not replicate the achievement of
Jesuits, hard though they tried.

This society needs economic pluralism for productive
efficiency, and it needs social and political pluralism to
counteract excessive tendencies to centralism. But above all,
it uses social and political pluralism, but of a special, modular,
ad hoc kind which does not stifle individuality, while at the
same time acting as a countervailing force to the centre.
Majority rule or representative institutions which symbolize
the equality of citizens through the one-man, one-vote rule
are an important contribution to all this, though they are
not of its very essence. What is essential to it is the absence
of either ideological or institutional monopoly: no one
doctrine is elevated to sacredness and uniquely linked to the
social order. Positions of power are rotated like all others
and do not attract incommensurate or even particularly
great rewards.

Theorists of democracy who operate in the abstract, without reference to concrete social conditions, end up with a
vindication of democracy as a general ideal, but are then
obliged to concede that in many societies the ideal is not
realizable. They end up with an ideal, universally vindicated in
some bizarre sense, but one which at the same time is quite

irrelevant to many, probably the very large majority of societies, because it is held to be inaccessible for them. Is it not better to include the pre-conditions in the notion of the desired order, and operate with something realistic, rather than with something absurdly abstract? The abstract model incidentally assumes one kind of man (the modern individualist, secular in outlook) and mistakenly treats him as man-in-general. An abstract vindication is offered first, and treated as universally valid; then it is regretfully conceded that the universal ideal, alas, cannot be implemented in most of the circumstances which have fallen to the lot of mankind. A curious kind of validity ... Is it not better to state the conditions which make the ideal feasible, or perhaps even mandatory, and start from that? 'Civil Society' is a more realistic notion, which specifies and includes its own conditions, rather than taking them for granted and then declaring itself unavailable for most of mankind through the absence of suitable pre-conditions . . .

So, although 'democracy' is indeed involved, it is the institutions and social context which alone make it possible and preferable that really matter. Without these institutional pre-conditions, 'democracy' has little clear meaning or feasibility. If the term is simply used as a code name for that set of institutions, then of course no harm is done. Because it highlights those institutional pre-conditions and the necessary historical context, 'Civil Society' is probably a better, more illuminating slogan than 'democracy'.

25

HISTORICAL OVERVIEW

There is a wide variety of ways in which human beings can arrange their social existence. For a long time, evidently, they lived in small intimate communities within which technology remained simple and the division of labour could not proceed very far. A generalization which one can hazard about such communities is this: within them, the problem of maintaining order and security trumped the desire for increasing production, even if (which is inherently improbable) the idea of a radical and sustained improvement in material conditions were present. These small communities could be more or less egalitarian, but they were generally participatory to the extent that the division of political labour also could not reach that level at which one could speak of the exclusion of a large proportion of the community from its political life. So, in that limited sense, such communities were democratic. We can say this in as far as they simply did not possess the organizational capacity for being radically, excessively inegalitarian.

This form of organization could reach certain levels of complexity. It could also in the end be supplemented by a different kind of polity, by large-scale units. These could either be built of communal elements, as when the central authority is a kind of powerful household or clan, or they can acquire a bureaucratic organization distinct from communal ones. A system of posts might arise independent of any one community, filled from the centre, and persisting over time even when the occupants change.

The religious and cognitive life of such societies is tied, on the one hand, to practical concerns, and on the other, to ritual activity. Ritual underscores and enforces social roles.

Society and religion, though they can become distinct, nevertheless remain closely linked. However, a major change comes in what some writers have called the Axial Age: the transcendent becomes conscious of itself as such, and disconnects itself from the social, or perhaps one should say, from any one particular form of the social.

One reason for this would seem to be the fact that the use of writing makes it possible and tempting to codify doctrine independently of any particular personnel or ritual. Writing gives ideas an independent, Platonic existence. The notion that ideas exist independently becomes plausible only if they exist independently of context, and that is a gift conferred on them by writing. An idea which is written down acquires an existence independent of the authority or identity of the speaker, who may indeed not be known. Writing constitutes the infrastructure of Platonism. Second, urbanization often creates populations living in disorganized conditions, who in distress can no longer turn to their communal segment – it may simply not be available – but instead are receptive to a kind of omnibus, open-to-all-comers promise of salvation, of recovery, whether in this or another world.

These conditions engender a new kind of religion, which is usually called world religion. There are religions which are half-way to being world faiths. Judaism had a universal deity but remained linked to an ethnic group. Hinduism is endowed with written doctrine but is incarnated in a socially specific communal organization without which it is unthinkable. But some religions, especially in their higher (as opposed to folk) version, have their centre of gravity in a message rather than a community or institution. It is then tied to a doctrine or a distinct point of revelation, but not tied to any one ethnic group or political organization, or to any pre-existent polity – though it may be linked to an organization which it itself sets up. In as far as its centre of gravity is in the doctrine which offers salvation, it tends to codify doctrine, and may create a sense of the importance of the boundary between orthodoxy and heresy, and faith and doubt and rival faith. Religion ceases to define the boundary of communities and defines the boundary of truth instead.

Through all this, a new kind of society becomes possible – an *Umma* or an ideocracy. This is a society which endeavours to implement an abstract model which it holds to be authoritative, an ideal which has an independent existence in writing. If a society is indeed defined by its faith, the boundary of the acceptance of doctrine becomes the boundary of the community. Society is then the shadow of faith; and we have an *Umma*. Such societies have often been referred to as theocracies, but it is useful to employ a broader term which conveys the fact that the idea which is being implemented may be, but need not always be, theistic. Quite often one also comes across mixed forms, i.e, partial efforts to implement abstract, normative ideals, co-existing in some kind of compromise with more mundane, communal organizations and practices. The Platonic or ideocratic element, the imposition of an abstract model on the social flesh, competes with the opposite tendency, the need of concrete social organization to express itself in ritual.

David Hume's generalization to the effect that communal organization with its priests is more favourable to liberty than societies inspired by and based on doctrinal enthusiasm is valid only provided one interprets 'liberty' in a sense which makes it compatible with the great ritual and communal obligations which pervaded, for instance, the world of classical antiquity. But that is not our freedom. More illumination can perhaps be obtained from Hume's other generalization (ironically in diametrical opposition to the first) to the effect that it is one particular kind of *Umma*, namely the one erected in north-west Europe by puritan enthusiasts, which in the end favoured liberty. (Although Hume did not say so, it was reproduced with remarkable long-term effects on the other side of the Atlantic, initially without even the benefit of industrialism, as was documented by Tocqueville not so long after Hume.) It is this type of society which really produced the kind of freedom which we now treasure, the modularity which lies at the base of Civil Society.

It is at this point that it becomes possible to talk about Civil Society. What is important is not merely the separation of the social and the economic, but the balance of power between the two. Something like the Ottoman state was also perfectly conscious of the distinction between the producers and the maintainers of order, and the same is true of Muslim states generally, but it would be difficult to credit them with Civil Society. In those kinds of society, it is only too clear who is boss. What distinguishes Civil Society (using the term to describe the entire society), or a society *containing* Civil Society (in the narrower sense), from others is that it is *not* clear who is boss. Civil Society can check and oppose the state. It is not supine before it. According to its most influential critic, Karl Marx, it is actually Civil Society which is boss, and the power of the state, or even its independence, is mere façade, a sham. This is the broader sense of Civil Society: it refers to a total society within which the non-political institutions are not dominated by the political ones, and do not stifle individuals either.

How on earth can a group or mass of people who, *ex hypothesi*, have shed their side arms (if ever they had any) counterbalance an institution which by definition more or less monopolizes arms and the habit of using them? What even contest could there possibly be between such parties, one so well equipped and trained, and the other, un-equipped and un-trained? Could there be the slightest doubt about the outcome? What absurdity is this? How could anyone even seriously ask such a question?

Well, the question is not absurd, and its answer not obvious. As it happens, in the Anglo-Saxon world, Civil

Society defeated the state not once but twice, in two successive centuries, in two civil wars pregnant with consequences for human history. It was the Roundheads who won the Civil War, and it was the Americans who won the War of Independence. Society defeated the state, the specialist in violence *par excellence*, in war.

One can answer the question only in part in terms of the military technology of the times. In the seventeenth and eighteenth centuries, the equipment improvised by the civil population which turned to rebellion in defence of its rights was not so very inferior, if inferior at all, to that available to the central forces. By the late twentieth century, the power of the weapons of the central army is so terrible that it can only be used by exceedingly ruthless and brutal authorities if confronted with widespread and cohesive opposition. But it is incomparably more potent than anything most societies can possibly improvise. It is also limited in its power in mountains or jungle, as Indo-China, Afghanistan and Algeria demonstrated. To be vulnerable to the weapon of civilization, you need yourself to be endowed with a civilized infrastructure . . .

But there is a more general answer. The state can still win, as is plausible in many or most cases, and often did so in outright confrontations. But, in a multi-state world gradually more and more subject to what might be called creeping economic growth, the victory was Pyrrhic. The powers of centralism, hierarchy, faith, an integrated society, have won two great if temporary victories in European history – the Counter-Reformation and Communism – and both proved catastrophic for the societies in which these victories occurred. One was the victory of the Counter-Reformation in southern Europe, and the other the victory of Bolshevism in Eastern Europe. It took much longer to undo the stagnation induced by the Jesuits than it took to undo the work of the Leninists: history and economic growth have accelerated and things move faster in the twentieth century than they did from the seventeenth to the nineteenth. But the pattern is the same: if the state defeats and destroys or subjugates Civil Society, in a wider plural world in which national wealth and its growth count for a very great deal, then the society as a whole pays the price, and in the end has to correct and reverse that disastrous victory, in pursuit of economic *rattrapage*. The first *rattrapage* has worked in the end, after a dubious start: by the late twentieth century, southern Europe has escaped from the Counter-Reformation.

One contrast involved in the notion of Civil Society is that between economic and social activities on the one hand and centralized order-maintaining ones on the other. The other contrast occurs at another and more general level, and is the contrast between societies in which this separation without subordination can take place and those in which it is lacking. It cannot occur in societies in which the power structure and the communal structure are in any case more or less identical; and it cannot occur in despotic empires in which naked power rules over communities; nor can it occur in societies in which economic and political rank are one. It cannot occur in societies, such as those described by Ibn Khaldun, in which the productive sector of society is indeed distinct from the political, but is atomized, helpless and supine. It cannot occur in an *Umma*, when the unique and exclusive sacralization of one faith makes pluralism impossible.

But before the notion of Civil Society could make the transition from being a somewhat dusty tool of academic analysis to becoming a genuinely rousing, powerful and resonant political slogan, something else also had to happen. Civil Society, previously contrasted with various forms of tribal, communal, feudal, oriental and perhaps other societies, also had to acquire a new and deadly contrast – a secular

Umma, and moreover one which was Caesaro-Papist-Mammonist, one inspired by a doctrine which, in the name of abolishing the political and sacralizing and freeing the economic, in fact unified and centralized the political, the economic and the ideological. It thereby extended that monopoly of coercion and command, which is in any case inherent in political organization under modern conditions, to the economic sphere. It was this disastrous experiment which propelled the phrase into the realm of luminous political ideals.

26

FUTURE PROSPECTS

What are the prospects for this type of social order?

The first thing to note is that the natural selection mechanism which worked in its favour so dramatically and conclusively in the past need no longer work for it, or at least not for it alone. It severely punished both the Counter-Reformation and Bolshevism: each of them had in its own way established a hierarchical, ideocratic society incapable of much effective economic competition, and each of them in due course suffered severely in consequence. But, by the twentieth century, the desirability of technologically sophisticated productive orientation has sunk in, and societies whose deepest instinct in the past was to reject innovation however efficient, in the interest of protecting social stability, no longer do so. On the contrary, many of them are fully aware that only with and through technological innovation and the economic benefits it brings can they maintain themselves in the condition to which they wish to become accustomed – and indeed maintain their social stability and their own traditions, which would otherwise be undermined by alien superiority.

This being so, we can now observe, especially in East Asia, societies whose economic performance is brilliant, which have adopted the new technology and some of its organizational accompaniments, but which are endowed with a spirit which is not individualistic, and which have not too much in common with the modular social ethos of Western Civil Society – and which, as far as one can tell, do not greatly mind this being so. Moreover, it no longer necessarily impedes their economic performance. It had once been held a truism of the sociology of industrial society that it required a flexible and mobile labour market, and that it was incompatible with the security provided by paternalism. The Japanese had already refuted this, possessing a brilliant economy whose enterprises are notorious for their 'feudal' or communal features, for the way in which they grant life-long security, respect seniority and hierarchy, and so forth.

Whatever may have been true of early industrialism, it would seem that late industrialism is compatible with a virtually feudal sense of loyalty and hierarchy. It would seem that once the great wealth-producing potential of new technology is properly appreciated, cultures which are inherently conservative, holistic and traditionalistic, nevertheless can and do overcome their aversion to something which brings in quite so much money, and can adapt themselves to it very successfully.

Individualism itself may also become redundant once the possibility and rewards of innovative enterprise become widely recognized, and accepted even by entire collectivities. Economic dynamism is incompatible with total centralization of the Bolshevik kind: it may be compatible with a looser, plural but strongly communal spirit. If this is so, the diffusion of Civil (i.e. individualist, modular) Society will no longer be underwritten by an economic variant of natural selection ... It may indeed have eliminated the Bolshevik *Umma*, but it does not eliminate social forms which have proved they can accommodate the new productive procedures, and often do it better than those who had initiated them. Bolshevism was undone not only by its failure to overtake Western capitalism, but also by the realization that someone else (i.e. East Asians) was capable of doing so. In the erstwhile USSR, the awareness that Western capitalism was indeed being overtaken but not by Marxism was a significant factor in the final abandonment of Communist faith. Social selection at present favours good economic performance: it is not yet clear to what extent liberalism and

Civil Society can continue to ride on the coat-tails of economic success.

So it seems perfectly possible to run a successful modern industrial society pervaded by a communalistic or family spirit with an authoritarian state presiding over it. Neither the lack of political and intellectual liberty, the lack of social liberty nor the perpetuation of a Confucian family spirit seems bound to inhibit economic performance. Whether we like it or not, the deadly angel who spells death to economic inefficiency is not always at the service of liberty. He had once rendered liberty some service, but does not seem permanently at her command. This may sadden those of us who are liberals and were pleased at being given such a potent ally – but facts had better be faced.

The case of Muslim societies has already been noted. What is interesting in their instance is not outstanding economic performance – their performance is middling, neither brilliant nor catastrophic, and it is hard to say what will happen after the exhaustion of oil reserves – but the fact that, as a result of the impact of modernization, they are well on the way to imposing an *Umma* in which a pre-industrial religion actually benefits from the conditions brought about by industrialization. The scripturalism, pervasive rule-orientation and puritanism, the regulation though not sacralization of economic life, the monotheism, restrained ritualism and religious though not political individualism, have somehow produced a world religion which, at any rate so far, is secularization-resistant, and tends increasingly to dominate the polities within which it has a majority. There is of course the curious case of Turkey, where the masses seem to take part in this trend, but have a plural Civil Society imposed on them by a military-political élite committed to a secular stance as part of the Kemalist heritage, of which it is the conscientious and sometimes ferocious guardian. It had initially adopted it as the supposed key to modernity and to political and military equality with the developed world, and has, with a most endearing stubbornness, clung to this association. This has led to a curious new cyclical system: implementation of democracy leads to a victory of pro-religious tendencies, which violate the Kemalist principles and provoke a corrective *coup*. After setting the house in order the generals step down, restore democracy and the cycle continues.

As far as the international scene is concerned, the prospects for Civil Society are moderately good, without at the same time providing any grounds for excessive complacency. The major industrial powers are adherents of it or converts, either by long tradition (Atlantic democracies), or by military defeat (the militaristic romantic nations, who learnt that more power is to be secured through trade and production than by the sword), or by economic defeat (Marxist Caesaro-Papism). The informal alliance of superpowers drawn from this general even if heterogeneous category can easily dominate the world and, as long as it is not too disunited, thwart attempts at blackmail or at the attainment of a position from which blackmail would be possible. They can live with the polities which do not share the spirit of Civil Society, as long as they themselves retain that dominance and minimal cohesion, and as long as the most recent cohort of effective industrializers continues to be interested in wealth and not much else.

27

INTERNAL PROBLEMS

The problems facing societies which are at present eager to set up Civil Society by fiat from above have been discussed, though of course not adequately. All one can do is repeat that the achievement within the span of a few years of something that had taken years of slow and occasionally painful and turbulent growth cannot be easy – though genuine encouragement can be found in the fact that there is indeed a strong and widespread yearning for the attainment of this condition. What seems to have happened almost accidentally in the West through the thwarting of an *Umma* of enthusiasts may yet come about in Eastern Europe through positive endeavour. A secular *Umma*-by-design has failed dramatically and unambiguously: a similarly intended compromise may yet succeed.

Civil Society also faces problems in its well-established original homelands. Montesquieu's remark that tyranny is based on human vices and liberty on human virtues is often quoted. The fact that it is not exclusively dependent on human virtues is no doubt something which enhances the prospects of Civil Society. It also finds its support in human traits which are relatively neutral, such as consumerism, capacity to routinize rather than take religious convictions too seriously, and others of the kind. Mandeville as well as Montesquieu is relevant: some private vices are public virtues, and Civil Society may find support in them. Nevertheless, it probably does require at least a measure of virtue, and it has been argued, for instance by Fred Hirsch[1] or earlier by David Riesman[2] and by W.H. Whyte,[3] that some of that rugged individualism which underlay a modular social order is fast running out. This may well be the case. On the other side, one may also accept the Weberian argument that virtues which could only initially emerge as the by-product of bizarre religious conviction, because their beneficent effects were not known and were anticipated by no one, nevertheless become habit-forming and are perpetuated, once their place in a modern economy is properly and widely understood.

There is also the interesting question of whether and to what extent Civil Society is dependent on the commitment to economic growth and thereby to an unstable occupational and social structure, with all that entails (and it entails a vast amount). Can economic growth continue for ever? If it ceases, can Civil Society survive it?

There is no reason to suppose that technical innovations should ever cease. It is however very plausible to suppose that the time is not too distant when further innovations can only make a very small impact on human well-being, or are liable to make an adverse one. As such time approaches, strife must inevitably shift from competition for material goods to competition for 'positional goods', in Fred Hirsch's phrase. In the more affluent industrial societies, at any rate in their better-off strata, the concern with material goods has in any case tended in effect to become a hidden concern with positional goods, i.e. relative status. Positional goods are *ex hypothesi* limited, and cannot really be increased by growth of material output.

Skilful manipulation of illusion can increase the supply of positional satisfaction a bit. For instance, I once took part in an academic debate which I was sure I had won, a fact which gave and still gives me some pleasure. I later discovered that my opponent was equally convinced that *he* had won that debate, and this gave *him* pleasure too. Perhaps we could not both be right but we could both be happy, and so the illusion enhanced the sum total of human happiness. To some extent, societies could institutionalize this kind of illusion: tennis players could be encouraged to believe that only proficiency in that game really makes a man admirable, while scholars would think the same about scholarship, womanizers about sexual conquest, and so on. In this way, lots and lots of people can feel that they and their group alone belong to the social élite, and remain untroubled by the fact that they rank rather badly by criteria which are paramount for others. To some extent, Civil Society with its multiplicity not only of activities but also of standards of excellence does indeed – and that is one of its charms – operate such a system of illusions, which allows quite a lot of people to believe themselves to be at the top of the ladder, because there are so many independent ladders, and each person can think that the ladder on which he is well placed is the one that really matters.

For all that, there are no doubt limits to the general contentment such delusions can engender. For centuries, liberal societies depended on growth for their legitimacy, though this has only recently been properly recognized. When growth ceases to be the basis of legitimacy, and when mobility ceases to be an imperative imposed by the pursuit of growth, it is eminently possible that society will revert to the condition which has characterized most societies, and complex ones most of all – a hierarchical system in which status is deeply internalized and pervades a whole range of activities. Without growth, mobility is a risky zero-sum game, in which anyone's gain is balanced by someone else's loss. Nothing much is gained in the aggregate, and instability is the price. To this must be added the consideration that in a mobile society everyone is liable to feel insecure. A status society might give security, and recover the feeling that society constitutes a moral order, something which was so unsuccessfully attempted by the Marxist *Umma*. Whether this will come about in a society based on a highly sophisti-cated technology and a high standard of living is something which remains to be seen. It is not a possibility one can ignore, and if it does come about, then Civil Society may once again disappear and be replaced by a rigid status order.

28

THE RANGE OF OPTIONS

If, initially, one operates with only two binary variables, one gets a two-by-two table. The variables were: 1) whether or not the economy is separate from the polity, and 2) whether or not coercion is concentrated.

Basic social order

	Coercion diffused	Coercion concentrated
Economy subordinate	Segmentary society STABLE, COMMON	Traditional, centralized, authoritarian state CYCLICAL, STABLE, COMMON
Economy separate and with high priority	Commercial city state UNSTABLE	Civil Society ?

The fusion of the two aspects of life, plus the primacy of political considerations, gives us something like the segmentary societies of the anthropologists. There, social units are at the same time productive ones, but their defence and the maintenance of internal order absolutely trump economic considerations. By contrast, the similar fusion of the two aspects, but with a much higher rating being accorded to economic activities, gives us the traditional commercial city state. Thirdly, the separation of the two aspects of life, with the polity dominant, gives us the traditional authoritarian state, tolerating a distinct and specialized economic sector, but firmly controlling it. The separation of the two, but with the economy not merely independent but actually dominant, treating the polity as its accountable servant, is Civil Society. Marxism made it a taunt that the bourgeois state was merely a kind of executive committee of the bourgeoisie: that this should even have become possible is perhaps mankind's greatest social achievement ever.

Civil Society should bear Marx's taunt as its greatest badge of honour. The taming of power, its reduction to an instrument, one to be judged by its effectiveness and service, rather than allowing it to be a master – this is perhaps mankind's greatest triumph. Marxists thought they would replace the dominance of the productive element in Civil Society by a genuine community: all they really achieved, and all that could be achieved by their method, was the return to the rule of coercion. Marxism had taught men to think in terms of a mistaken polarity – the contrast between individualism and communalism. The really relevant opposition is between the rule of coercers and the rule of producers. Marxism had simply re-established the rule of coercion in the name of collectivism.

Of the four species, two – segmentary societies and authoritarian states – are hardy plants frequently found all over the globe and in a wide variety of periods. By contrast, commercial city states are brilliant but highly unstable and seldom survive for very long. They were marked by that class conflict which Marxism claimed to be the general condition of *all* human societies, except for the first and the last. And the last of our four social forms, Civil Society, has so far only come into being once, but at the moment looks as if it may conquer the world. Societies which exemplify it at least in some measure are richer and more powerful than those which do not. For all that, it may well be highly precarious like its apparent predecessor, the commercial city state.

That it should ever have come into being is a great miracle. The general situation of agrarian society does indeed have all the features which the Enlightenment attributed to medieval darkness: because faith is obscurantist, intellectual life is most often miserable, and economic improvement generally non-existent. Because there is no economic growth, limitation of available resources makes the general situation Malthusian, and so the perfectly rational concern of everyone is with their position in the structure, rather than with its overall performance. This in turn keeps the belief system obscurantist. Inevitably ruthless competition leads to oppressive and tyrannical political systems, in as far as tolerance would simply lead to the replacement of rulers by rivals, who would not be so foolish as to repeat the weakness of their predecessors. So priests and kings dominate. The Enlightenment was right in the picture it drew, but misguided in its starry-eyed illusion that it was all an avoidable mistake. It was nothing of the kind: it was inscribed in the nature of things.

The fourfold typology which we have set up here, and which follows from working out the implication of two simple but supremely important dichotomies, is incomplete. One further binary opposition must be introduced, which admittedly makes the model awkward by making it three-dimensional, and hence not easily presentable on two-dimensional paper. Nevertheless, it must be done. The further dimension is to be added not merely because it gives us a richer and more illuminating typology. It is also related to the puzzling problems raised above: how could we ever escape from the locked, closed vicious circle of agrarian life, from the self-perpetuation of tyranny and superstition? An ideologically high-pitch version of a social order, even if miserable, may explain a certain mysterious historical transition, the 'passing of a hump'.

Ideocratic versions of basic social types

	Coercion diffused	Coercion concentrated
Economy	Sparta	Islamic state
subordinate	VERY RARE	STABLE IF CYCLICAL, COMMON
Economy separate	Calvin/Knox type	Marxist ideocracy
and with	of religious polity	EVIDENTLY
high priority	UNSTABLE	UNSTABLE

This new dimension is the presence and intensity of abstract, principled *faith*. The initial polarization depended roughly on whether men are motivated by *honour* or by *interest*. Coercers live by honour, producers by interest. But some men follow neither of these two masters, or not altogether, and are possessed by the craving for virtue or salvation instead. This adds a third dimension. It is engendered by the use of social order to impose principles, and their use in turn to maintain social order. Each of four types of society initially engendered by the first, simpler, two-by-two model exemplifies a condition in which faith is none too intense, and does not burn with an unduly fierce flame. That typology ignored faith, because it is none too powerful in the four types in question. But it is important that man is also an ideological animal, capable of great intensity of faith. Dominion of faith, as the pursuit of salvation through virtue, engenders further social forms.

Corresponding to each of the four doctrinally low-keyed social forms, there is an enthusiast variant, endowed with the same mix of the other two variables as its corresponding (low-keyed) version, but being in addition smitten with faith. For ordinary segmentary society, the corresponding faith-intoxicated variant is Sparta, where, in Xenophon's words which so impressed Adam Ferguson, virtue is the business of the state. The faith-smitten social form corresponding to the commercial city state is something like Calvin's Geneva or John Knox's Scotland. It forcefully illustrates Hume's observation that puritan enthusiasm is a greater danger to liberty than the superstition of priests. Corresponding to the ordinary authoritarian agrarian state, the faith-governed version is well exemplified by Islam: here the faith has become politically disembodied, it can live on without the state, and sit in judgement on it. It is no longer linked to and permanently controlled by any one political authority, being incarnated in a transcendent law preserved in writing instead and in the keeping of a trans-polity and trans-ethnic clerical class, which, if the law is defied, can in alliance with communal forces on the edge of society restore the moral order. So in a sense faith dominates the state while remaining independent of it, even though the state is authoritarian and normally brooks no rivals in the sphere of coercion, in the territory it actually controls. Though specialists on the law may be individually or even collectively powerless, yet the ethos they transmit dominates society and imposes itself even on the state. Political authority can neither change it nor even manipulate it to any great extent. This solution to the question of how to run society worked well enough in the traditional agrarian world, and contrary to expectation is working even better now: Islam has grown stronger and purer in the last hundred years. It would be foolish to be dogmatic about whether this will continue. If indeed it does, then Islam will constitute a permanent and serious alternative to sceptical Civil Society, and we shall have this option of a fully industrial, computerized *Umma*.

And what is the faith-imbued alternative to the mix embodied in lukewarm form (and essentially, inherently lukewarm) in Civil Society? The answer: the Marxist world, as we have known it in its actual political incarnation between 1917 and its total collapse (at any rate in Europe) in 1989. Like Civil Society, it understood and recognized the difference between production and power, and the productive and political units were not identical, even if subjected to one and the same authority. According to its formal ideology and ultimate aims, the polity was to serve production: the essence of man was work, not domination and hierarchy. But in practice the running of society was subjected to a faith, and the business of state, as in Sparta, or in Calvin's Geneva, or in puritan Islam, was virtue. The consequence was a ruthless and centralized ideocracy.

The resulting Great Contest or cold war was unique in a number of ways: it was the first war fought under the new rules, basically by economic competition only (with relatively minor side conflicts in the form of peripheral wars-by-proxy). Moreover, it was a war which ended with an astonishingly clear, vivid verdict. It is interesting that the first war fought not on the battlefield but by competing productivity ended in such a conclusive, unambiguous victory for one side. In this war, unlike the one between the production and the warrior ethos which ended in 1945, the victors did not insist on unconditional surrender – but the losers conceded it without even being asked to do so. Never before had an ideological contest ended with such unanimity.

So the revival of the notion and ideal of Civil Society is of course intimately connected with the *Krach* of the Marxist system, and its preceding long, deep and bitter malaise. It is this collapse which has taught us how better to understand the logic of our situation, the nature of our previously half-felt, half-understood values. We now see the manner in which they emerge from the underlying constraints and strains of our condition. It provides a better way of understanding society and its basic general options.

29

VALIDATION?

Civil Society is a notion which serves a double function: it helps us understand how a given society actually works, and how it differs from alternative forms of social organization. It is a society in which polity and economy are distinct, where polity is instrumental but can and does check extremes of individual interest, but where the state in turn is checked by institutions with an economic base; it relies on economic growth which, by requiring cognitive growth, makes ideological monopoly impossible. This is its location on the map of possible forms of social organization. It seems to have historic roots in the city state and in the political centralization of the authoritarian state, and even on a thwarted but not wholly eroded aspiration for an *Umma*. It is a social form among others: preaching it in conditions which do not permit it is pointless.

At the same time, 'Civil Society' does help us clarify our social norms, and make plain what it is we endorse and why it appeals to us. In this respect, 'Civil Society' is markedly superior to a notion such as 'democracy', which, though it may highlight the fact that we prefer consent over coercion, tells us precious little concerning the social pre-conditions of the effectiveness of general consent and participation. It lumps together participatory tribal segments, ancient or medieval city states and modern growth-oriented national or supra-national states, obscuring the profound differences, whether in states of mind, social organization or external circumstance, under which these various forms operate or operated. By contrast, the notion of Civil Society highlights not only the mechanics but also the charms of the kind of society to which we aspire.

Civil Society is based on the separation of the polity from economic and social life (from, in effect, Civil Society in the narrower sense, i.e. the social residue left when the state is subtracted), but this is combined with the absence of domination of social life by the power-wielders, an absence so strange and barely imaginable in the traditional agrarian world, and found so surprising and precarious by Adam Ferguson. The political centralism is essential, for in the modern world economic and social units simply cannot double up as order-maintaining ones. Economic pluralism, far from total, is compatible with political control over strategic economic issues (indeed, requires this). The autonomy of the economy is needed, not merely in the name of efficiency (this would not matter too much, given that modern technology is in any case terrifyingly effective), but so as to provide pluralism with a social base which it cannot any longer find anywhere else. It requires intellectual or ideological pluralism: the growing economy which is indispensable to the system is impossible without science, and science is incompatible with a cognitive picture of the world which is socially sustained, enforced and endowed with *a priori* authority.

In the future, it may well need to operate in conditions which differ from those which originally helped to bring it into being. A central world political authority may come about and be indispensable, if ecological or terrorist disaster is to be avoided. This means that Civil Society will no longer benefit from the support of social-natural selection in a multi-state world, which had helped it so crucially in the past (even assuming that we can rely on efficiency continuing to be on its side, which is not obvious). It remains to be seen whether mere economic and cultural competition will have the same effect, and will suffice. Modularity/individualism may decline with the erosion of the faith which engendered it, and non-individualist cultures may surpass individualist ones economically: thus individualism may lose the vindication-by-wealth.

Cultural homogeneity will probably be severely disturbed by emigration engendered by differences of economic level, and put liberal politics under severe strain.

Why should we want Civil Society? Karl Popper, in *The Open Society and Its Enemies*[1] (a book to which the subtitle of the present work is an allusion), familiarized us with the difference between what he called 'historicist' and liberal ways of validating social arrangements. By 'historicism' he meant an appeal to the allegedly irreversible verdict of history: that which must be, is right. I am of course familiar with all the objections to historicism, not least because I was profoundly influenced by Popper's book: the verdicts of history are in fact most unclear and unpredictable, and even if one did know them it would still be craven to treat them as authoritative.

Nevertheless, I feel that a partial historicism is inevitable. Civil Society may or may not be the unique social corollary of the kind of scientific-industrial mode of life to which mankind is now ineluctably wedded; but at any rate a certain number of the visible and advertised alternatives to it are unlikely to be compatible with it. That consideration must be present in our mind.

So, all in all, Civil Society is justified at least in part by the fact that it seems linked to our historical destiny. A return to stagnant traditional agrarian society is not possible; so, industrialism being our manifest destiny, we are thereby also committed to its social corollaries. On top of that, we – or some of us – also actually like it: we have no desire to live under an ideocracy, old-style or new, or under some kind of traditional communitarianism, let alone under the old central-ized authoritarian regimes. But we are the fruit of that which we also endorse, and how much does our endorsement add to its merits? Something, perhaps the collapse of Marxist ideocracy, demonstrates that modern man is not slave even to the most persistent and monopolistic indoctrination, and does not necessarily like that which pervades his world even though for a time it seems to have no alternative and be endowed with a powerful self-validating rationale. But what point is there in vaunting our values, and condemning the commitment of others to absolutist transcendentalism or demanding communalism? They are what they are, and we are what we are: if we were them, we would have their values, and if they were us, they would have ours. I am not a relativist − the existence of a culture-transcending truth seems to me the most important single fact about the human condition, and indeed one of the bases of Civil Society, for it made possible that cognitive growth and the denial of absolutism on which it is based. But all the same, preaching across cultural boundaries seems to me in most circumstances a fairly pointless exercise.

In some limited measure, therefore, our attachment to Civil Society does have a kind of historicist foundation. But not altogether. Historical circumstances may eliminate some of its rivals, but in all probability they do not uniquely determine the residue (and most certainly do not determine it in all its details). Within the range of options which then remains − and we do not yet know just what that range is − the choice is ours. The code of cognitive conduct which has emerged with Civil Society, which separates facts and values, unfortunately prevents us from terminating the regress of justifications, and freeing our choice from the charge of arbitrariness. But that is our situation, and we cannot escape it. My own choice happens to be clear, but the nature of our values also prevents us from validating it. A validation of the choice would require that it be the corollary of an absolutized and unique vision: yet the rules of the order we choose forbid precisely such an absolutization! So the nature of our choice prevents us from proving its pre-eminent merit. We have to live with this. Paraphrasing Kant on

ethics, we cannot overcome this tension, but we can understand why we must suffer it. Do not blame the bearer of the
news for its content.

NOTES

1. A SLOGAN IS BORN

1. Fustel de Coulanges, *La Cité Antique,* Paris, 1864; reprinted Paris, 1967.
2. ibid., p. 2.
3. 'Liberty of the Ancients compared with that of the Moderns', in Benjamin Constant, *Political Writings*, B. Fontana (ed.), Cambridge, 1988, pp. 308–29.
4. Fustel de Coulanges, op. cit., p. 265.
5. Cf. Louis Dumont, *From Mandeville to Marx*, Chicago, 1977.
6. Emile Masqueray, *Formation des Cités Chez les Populations Sédentaires de l'Algérie*, Paris, 1886; reprinted Aix-en-Provence, 1983, F. Colonna (ed.).
7. Robert I. Levy, *Mesocosm*, Berkeley, 1990, p. 21.
8. There is an excellent survey of the discussion and relevance of the actions of Civil Society by John Keane, Andrew Arato, Pierre Rosenvallon, Jacques Rupnik, Adam Michnik, Elmer Hankiss and others, in Krishnan Kumar, 'Civil Society; an inquiry into the usefulness of an historical term', in *The British Journal of Sociology*, vol. 44, no. 3 (September 1993). See also Dominique Colas, 'Le Glaive et le Fléau, Généalogie du Fanatisme et de la Société Civile', Grasset (ed.), 1992; *Civil Society and the State: New European Perspectives,* John Keane (ed.), London, 1988; and *Market Economy and Civil Society in Hungary*, C. M. Hann (ed.), London, 1990.

3. ISLAM

1. *Marxisme et Algérie, Textes de Marx–Engels*, Galissot and Badia (eds.), Paris, 1976.
2. Cf. Gilles Kepel, *The Revenge of God*, Alan Bruley (trans.), Cambridge, 1993.

4. THE MARXIST FAILURE

1. Roman Szporluk, *Communism and Nationalism. Karl Marx versus Friedrich List*, Oxford and New York, 1988.
2. Christel Lane, *The Rites of Rulers: Ritual in Industrial Society – The Soviet Case*, Cambridge, 1981.

5. THE SUCCESSFUL *UMMA*

1. David Hume, *The Natural History of Religion*, A. Wayne Colver (ed.), Oxford, 1976, chapter XI.
2. ibid., chapter IX.
3. David Hume, 'Of Superstition and Enthusiasm', in *Essays Moral, Political and Literary*, Oxford, 1963. Also in *Hume on Religion*, R. Wollheim (ed.), London, 1963.

7. CIVIL SOCIETY COMPLETES THE CIRCLE

1. Leszek Kolakowski, 'The Myth of Human Self-Identity: Unity of Civil and Political Society in Socialist Thought', originally published in *The Socialist Idea: A Reappraisal*, L. Kolakowski and S. Hampshire (eds.), London, 1974; and re-published in *The Transition from Socialism*, C. Kukathas, D.W. Lovell and W. Malley (eds.), Melbourne, 1991.
2 ibid., p. 49.
3. ibid., p. 57.
4. ibid., p. 57.

8. ADAM FERGUSON

1. Adam Ferguson, *An Essay on the History of Civil Society* (4th edn, revised and corrected, London, 1773), reprinted Farnborough, 1969.
2. ibid., p. 114.
3. Emile Durkheim, *De la Division du Travail Social,* Paris, 1902.
4. Ferguson, op. cit., p. 384.
5. ibid.
6. ibid., p. 387.
7. Ibn Khaldun, *Muqaddima*, F. Rosenthal (trans.), London, 1958.
8. Ferguson, op. cit., p. 244.
9. ibid., p. 228.

10. ibid., p. 385.
11. ibid.
12. ibid., p. 251.
13. ibid., pp. 251–2.
14. Ferguson's preoccupation with this point was inspired in part by the exclusion of Scots from the raising of militias against a possible French invasion – an exclusion inspired, of course, by the fear of placing arms in Jacobite hands. I owe this point to a personal communication from Professor Marilyn Butler.
15. J. Burckhardt, *Weltgeschichtliche Betrachtungen*, Historiche Fragmente aus dem nachlass/herausgegeben von Albert Deri und Emil Durr. Stuttgart, 1929.
16. Ferguson, op. cit., pp. 220–21.
17. ibid., p. 267.
18. ibid.
19. Cf. John Hall in *Europe and the Rise of Capitalism*, Jean Baechler, John Hall and Michael Mann (eds.), Oxford and New York, 1988.
20. E. A. Wrigley, *People, Cities and Wealth: The Transformation of Traditional Society*, Oxford, 1987.

9. EAST IS EAST AND WEST IS WEST

1. Personal communication from Shireen Khazeni, on the basis of her researches into nineteenth-century Persia.
2. Perry Anderson, *The Lineages of the Absolute State*, London 1974, p. 94.

10. POLITICAL CENTRALIZATION AND ECONOMIC DECENTRALIZATION

1. Václav Havel, *Power of the Powerless*, Armonk, NY, 1990.

14. FRIEND OR FOE?

1. James Hogg, *The Private Memoirs and Confessions of a Justified Sinner*, London, 1824; John Wain (ed.), Harmondsworth, 1983.

15. THE TIME ZONES OF EUROPE

1. 'Qu'est-ce qu'une Nation?' in *Ernest Renan et l'Allemagne*, E. Burem (ed.), New York, 1945.

2. Cf. Miroslav Hroch, *Social Preconditions of National Revival in Europe*, Cambridge, 1985.
3. Cf. Conor Cruise O'Brien, *God Land: Reflections on Religion and Nationalism*, London, 1988.

27. INTERNAL PROBLEMS

1. F. Hirsch, *The Social Limits of Growth*, London, 1977.
2. David Riesman, *The Lonely Crowd*, New Haven, 1961.
3. W. H. Whyte, *The Organization Man*, Harmondsworth, 1960.

29. VALIDATION?

1. Karl Popper, *The Open Society and its Enemies* (5th edn), Princeton, 1966.

INDEX